Words of Praise for *Common People Uncommon Lives*:

"Jan has the unique talent of taking snippets of life and putting them together in a marvelous way that brings a lump to the throat, tears to the eyes, or an understanding chuckle. Her stories are told simply and with great understanding, and indeed, tell the story of common people, uncommon lives."

Dave Eddy
WBCK Radio, Battle Creek's "Morning Mayor"

"… takes me back in time to when common people who did uncommon things were valued not because of their education or degrees, but because of their love for family. You see parts of your family and your story here. I feel privileged to have read this book."

Harry Bonner Sr.
4-H Leader, Volunteer, Michigan 4-H Youth Development

"…touching and uplifting. These stories remind us once again of the unparalleled blessings we receive with the opportunity to live in America – among Americans."

Michael Medved
Nationally Syndicated Radio Host, Author, *Saving Childhood*

"In the years it's been my joy to know Jan Corey Arnett, I've admired her for many things, most of all her gift for friendship. The very old and the very young, the high achievers and the nobodies, the gracious and the cranky – to them all, Jan brings a perceptive eye, a listening ear, and a caring heart. In *Common People Uncommon Lives* you'll meet fascinating folks who'll become your own friends too. Best of all, you'll learn from this compassionate observer of the human scene to look a little closer at the people who cross your own path each day. Companionship, joy and wisdom, Jan shows us, are as close as the next person you meet."

Elizabeth Sherrill
Author, *All the Way to Heaven*

"Reading *Common People Uncommon Lives* is like sitting at Jan's kitchen table and hearing warm rich accounts of her childhood and fascinating circle of friends. Jan's gentle humor and compassionate spirit infuse each essay, providing inspiration, amusement, and just plain good reading."

Linda Jo Scott
Professor Emerita, Olivet College, Michigan

"Jan Corey Arnett draws us into her world with stories of struggle and hope, love and laughter. Her writing celebrates relationships that bring inspiration, encouragement, wisdom, and comfort into our lives. In the honest, 'over the back fence' language of neighbors and friends, she helps us discover the extraordinary in the ordinary."

Sarah Briggs
Editor, Albion College, Michigan

Common
People
Uncommon
Lives

Jan Corey Arnett

Coralan
Press
Battle Creek, MI

Dedicated to:

my father, Ken Corey,
who taught me to save the stories that matter;
my mother, Mille Corey,
who notices the nuances that make the natural world a place
of enchantment;
and, to my sister, Sue Corey,
whose courage and compassion, grit and grace, amaze and inspire me.

Published by Coralan Press
2444 W. Halbert Rd.
Battle Creek, MI 49017
www.jancoreyarnett.com

Publisher's Cataloguing-in Publication Data
Arnett, Jan Corey

      Common people, uncommon lives / Jan Corey Arnett. --Battle Creek, MI : Coralan Press, 2003.

        p. ; cm.
        ISBN: 0-9729648-1-9

        1. Anecdotes. I. Title.

PN6261 .A76 2003   2003104278
808.88/2--dc21   0309

Back cover photo by Phaff Studio, Battle Creek, Michigan

Printed in the United States of America

07 06 05 04 03 • 5 4 3 2 1

Contents

My Mare and Me
I have an old mare. You can tell by her hair.
And though she is old I love her still.
Together we stand upon a hill.
My mare and me.

I swim in the river while she stands under a tree.
We suit ourselves as you can see.
But we love each other.
My mare and me.

Introduction and Acknowledgments

As a child of seven or eight, I had written a simple poem about my imaginary horse. My parents, Ken and Mille Corey, and sisters, Judy, Sue, June, and Lois, praised me profusely as loving families do. My teacher said it demonstrated a special flair (I wasn't sure what that meant). The kudos bolstered my fragile young ego and validated me as a person, though I could not have articulated it in that way at that age. Nor could I have explained that the rhythm of the words gave voice to feelings, and the feelings once committed to paper had permanence. All I knew was that what I had done mattered, and because of it I wanted to be a writer.

I have moved through my career experience as a newspaper reporter, magazine editor, technical writer, and photographer. This work has made a living. It has taught me to ask questions and to dig for the story that lies beneath the press release, and the pomp and circumstance.

I have traveled through my life experience as a journal-keeper, story-teller, and image-maker, drawn over and over to stories which explore emotions, perseverance, old-fashioned values, and the spirituality that emanates from our kinship with the earth, one another, and with a universal spirit-energy-creator-god. This work has made a life. It has taught me to seek the divine in joyful simplicity. My relationships with the earth and those who cherish it renew my spirit, because it is through them that I come closest to touching our Creator.

children who have an innate ability to push the limits of an adult's endurance — even those of us who were new to adulthood.

Bill helped all of us to appreciate the value of being tested. "God has many ways to teach us," he would say.

Every Child Needs Love. It was easy to tell the repeat campers from the first-timers. The repeat campers could hardly wait for their parents to leave so that they could launch full-tilt into the week ahead, galloping off to the cabins, the dining hall, or the beach as if they owned the place. The first-timers, particularly the youngest children away from home for the first time alone, lingered anxiously beside a mother or father, the week seeming to stretch ahead like eternity. Homesick tears and a wet bed or two could be counted on, but a word slipped quietly to Bill at breakfast allowed a wet mattress to be removed and exchanged while everyone was away from the cabin. No child was embarrassed in front of peers.

The cure for a case of homesickness was a sheltering hug and a promise from Bill that he would personally look out for them for that great long week. He was the world's best substitute grandpa, one week at a time.

Some of the junior high, just-turned-teens often delighted in challenging authority, reminding me more than once of young livestock checking the pasture fence line for a place they might slip through, or butting heads to establish rank within the herd. One such boy in my group the summer of 1972, was Danny, a street-wise youngster from Detroit. From a quiet U.P. town with a population of fewer than a thousand and not yet twenty years old myself, I didn't know anything about Detroit or the ways of the street. Even so, as counselors we didn't have to concern ourselves back then with the whole issue of juvenile violence in the way that we might today. For us, a troubled youth was one whose vocabulary included an occasional cuss word or who did his level best to appear sure of himself, often a sure sign that he was anything but. Sometimes a troubled youngster was merely one with a continually sullen attitude who appeared uninterested in everything and everyone, but in fact wasn't missing a thing. It usually didn't take more than a day or two to bring these kids around, engaging them happily in the camp experience. Swimming in clear water, relaxing under sheltering trees, savoring Ma Tooley's huge brownies, and singing beside campfires, under a night sky liberally sprinkled with stars, has a way of softening the rough edges of teenage bravado.

Back then if teens wanted to carry a pocket knife while at camp that was fine, provided they knew how to use it safely for whittling wood or cutting rope. If they didn't, we showed them, then kept an eye on them to be sure the knife came out of their pockets only when we gave the okay. Rarely did any of the campers even own a pocket knife. But Danny from Detroit did.

One evening, the group of about sixteen boys and girls for which a male co-counselor and I were responsible, gathered around our campfire. We were preparing to spend the night camped out in sleeping bags near the lake rather than in our cabins. It was early evening, brilliantly-golden beams of light shone between the trees like spotlights on a stage. Danny crouched by the fire, pulled his knife from his pocket, opened it, rubbed the blade against his pantleg, and then held the tip of the blade over glowing coals.

"What are you doing that for, Danny?" I asked him in a deliberately casual voice, not wanting to provoke him into misbehaving to get more of the attention that I knew he already craved.

"Dunno," Danny said, "just playin'."

"You'd better be very careful. That blade will get hot before you even realize it and you can get badly burned in a hurry," I warned. "You'd best not leave it there long and don't touch it until it cools down." I wanted nothing in my voice to sound anxious or distrusting.

"Yah, I know," he replied vacantly, staring intently at the blade as he slowly turned it over and over just at the edge of the coals. He was being aloof, seemingly lost in his own thoughts as he had been since arriving at camp three days earlier. Danny did not want to let himself be drawn fully into his circle of peers, although there were moments when he seemed about to laugh with us instead of at us, or as if he wanted to join the conversation, then clammed up at the last moment.

Momentarily distracted by the needs of another camper, I glanced away. In an instant, my attention was painfully riveted entirely on myself. Danny had pressed the red-hot tip of the knife to my bare leg, just above the knee. I screamed in pain as he pulled it back, my seared flesh with it. A water blister appeared almost instantly. Danny hooted with devilish laughter as my co-counselor snatched the knife, took him by the shoulders, and marched him off for a little conversation with Bill Hampton.

Whether Danny realized the injury his actions would cause or whether he was just naively curious was unclear, but Bill Hampton was concerned not just about Danny's reaction to the incident, but about mine as well. Each of us would have our own emotions, none of them good.

"Every child deserves a chance," Bill said as he searched my face to gauge my feelings about Danny. I was seething with resentment toward this testy teen who kept all of us on guard.

"You should know that it was with some reluctance that Michigamme even accepted Danny into camp this year," Bill explained in a steady, even tone of voice. "He has a difficult family situation and what he needs right now is love. We still have to give him love. Can you do that, Jan?"

It was difficult, very difficult to feel loving toward Danny the remainder of the week as I changed the dressing on the burn, knowing it would likely leave a scar. I wanted to hate him, and each time he laughed in the devilish way he had at the campfire, anger welled up inside me. Over and over I had to remind myself of Bill's words. *What Danny needs is love.*

Throughout the entire week, as Bill went about his work tending the buildings, grounds, and daily workflow of the camp, he paid special attention to Danny and tried to reinforce the good in him. He would just as readily turn to me and whisper, "Remember how lucky you are to have the love of your parents. Danny doesn't know how to give love so that he can get love. Show him."

Danny made no dramatic improvements that week at Michigamme and I cannot honestly say that I was sad to see him leave, except to know that this confused boy was not returning to a home warmed by love.

The burn on my leg eventually healed, leaving a small triangular scar. Each time I see it, I am reminded of Bill's challenge to love when loving is hard to do. How much easier it is to love those who make loving easy.

Lord, Grant Me Patience. Each group of campers – elementary, junior high, or senior high – presents its own special array of needs, joys, and opportunities from which a counselor can learn.

The oldest teens, more so than younger children, want to appear to be sure of themselves and of everything around them. But underneath, nearly all struggle with the same insecurities – being accepted, fitting in, and doing as well as others.

Group discussions about dating, making ethical decisions, facing peer pressure with faith, usually start out awkwardly, but become increasingly animated. The teens begin to open up to one another as they realize they share so many fears and confusions.

Now and then, as Bill had time between camp chores or happened to be passing by en route to a leaky faucet or burned-out light bulb, he would sit in on our group discussions. Always, when he offered an observation or shared a belief, the kids were attentive. There was something in the humble, non-judgmental way he spoke, that conveyed a message as important as the words themselves. He could say, without saying, that he trusted these young people to do what was right and that he valued each and every one of them.

When I was a counselor during the summer of 1973, it was with senior high campers. It did not take long that summer, for the counselors and Bill to realize that there was one girl at the senior high camp who was different from all the rest. Pamela was a big-boned girl. Like many her age, she had facial blemishes that she tried hard to hide under pancake make-up or behind a nervous hand that seemed perpetually in motion. She wanted very much to fit in and to be accepted by her peers, but the harder she tried, the more they withdrew from her.

It wasn't her appearance, however, that made Pamela a loner. It was her tragic array of tics. I knew nothing about Tourette's Syndrome, which can cause a person to suffer from uncontrollable twitches, spasms, vocal sounds, and even outbursts of profanity. Pamela did not swear, which was fortunate in a church camp setting, but she could not talk without gruffly clearing her throat or making unpleasant snorting sounds. She stuttered and stammered. Her shoulders often twitched and she shifted from one foot to the other, scrunching up her nose, squinting her eyes, and running her hands under her nose or through her hair. She talked incessantly in run-on, broken sentences.

Pamela's tics made everyone anxious, as if they were contagious and we might all begin to have them ourselves. Sadly, it was only a matter of hours into the week that the girls in my group began to shun her.

Befriending one camper in a group more than the others or forming mini-cliques is common among kids. But for an entire group to completely ostracize one of its members is not. The more they avoided Pamela, the harder she tried to be accepted, which only made them seek even more ways to shut her out. Finally, she gave up on her peers and attached herself to me like a barnacle to a ship. As the adult responsible for this impressionable group of young ladies, it was my job to model patience, compassion, and kindness. But I discovered entirely too soon, that what I needed was in desperately short supply. If ever there was a time when the expression "Lord grant me patience, but I need it now!" fit the situation, this was it.

The moment the camp bell sounded to let us know it was time to roll out of our bunks and get ready for the day, Pamela started talking and coughing, wiggling and twitching. Before we left the cabin to walk to the dining hall, I felt myself tensing up, suppressing the urge to shout, "Pamela, stop it!" telling myself over and over that she couldn't help herself. Sometimes I rambled on about something, anything, in what I hoped was a calming tone of voice, just to try to have her stop talking for a few minutes. But barely had I finished a sentence when she'd interrupt and resume her compulsive chattering.

Oh, for just a few minutes of solitude! Just a few minutes without her talking at me! The desire for peace and quiet became overpowering.

I began searching for ways to get away from Pamela for even a few minutes, envying the teens as they continued to avoid her.

The restroom! If I could stay there a bit longer than necessary....

But even that strategy offered no reprieve. If I excused myself from the group during song time or crafts, Pamela would leave with me, standing outside the stall, raising her voice to compensate for the door between us, and continue chattering, snorting, and shuffling.

I had never encountered anything like this in my young life. The week stretched ahead, longer than the eternity it seemed to the frightened first-time campers.

I sought out Bill. In his ever-understanding, compassionate way, he looked into my eyes, just as I had seen him do so many times with the children, and gave me the advice I knew I needed to hear but was having a hard time putting into practice.

"God loves Pamela too, Jan," he said, in a soothing soft voice. "You must do your very best to be patient with her, listen to her troubles, and not allow the others to hurt her feelings. She cannot help herself. You must be the friend she so desperately craves."

I knew he was right. Oh, how I knew Bill was right. The more I tried to be patient and affectionate with Pamela, the more she clung to me. I felt suffocated, edgy, and most of all, angry at myself for my attitude. She couldn't help herself and if I wanted to get away from her problems, how much more must she wish to be free of them? Where was my compassion and empathy? Where was my ability to put myself in her shoes even for a moment?

At mealtime, Pamela sat beside me and jabbered incessantly. At evening campfire time, she wanted the place nearest me on the log benches that encircled the fire. When we hiked, she was on my heels keeping up a running ramble. It was only when lights-out came in the stillness of the cabin or when I had leadership duties that necessitated leaving my group with the other counselor for a short time during the day, that I could be alone with my own thoughts. I relished them as much as she relished companionship. Silence had never sounded so incredibly wonderful.

It was a difficult and trying week. God tested me and I didn't feel I had made the grade. It was a miserable feeling.

As Pamela's father put her suitcase into the trunk of his car that Saturday morning when senior high camp drew to a close, she hugged me so hard I could barely get my breath.

"I will write to you!" she chirped. "Will you write to me?"

"Yes I will," I nodded as she continued to cling to me.

"Promise me?"

"I promise."

We hugged again and I told her what a great young lady she was, because truly, underneath all that jerking and twitching, was a girl with a loving spirit.

We waved to one another as her father's big car headed out the gravel driveway and turned onto the road leading away from Camp Michigamme, back to the city that Pamela called home. Despite all the commotion from other campers bubbling to their parents, it was quiet. Enormously quiet, and curiously I wasn't sure how I felt about it.

"She's a girl with a lot of tough times ahead," Bill Hampton said, taking note of my awkwardness, "but Pamela's bright, she's got potential, and she will turn out all right."

True to her word, Pamela wrote to me. She must have barely unpacked her bags before she sat down to write the first of many letters. A high school photo arrived on the back of which was written,

> "You have done so much for me, O Lord,
> No wonder I am glad! I sing for joy." Psalms 92:4
>
> *Dear Jan*
> *Always be as joyful and life-loving and full of spirit as you*
> *were at Michigamme.*
> *Your friend, 4-ever and a day, PJ*

The girl in the photo was sunshiny with a face that radiated happiness. Pamela's kind words were much more a statement of what was good within her than anything that I deserved.

Pam graduated from high school and traveled all the way from Upper Michigan to Texas to attend a large university where she majored in music and religion. Eventually the awkward teenager whose unfortunate tics had caused her so much anxiety, married and became a Methodist minister. I was surprised when I learned this, but Bill Hampton was not. He had noticed something about her that I had missed in my inability to see beyond her problems. He had seen that spark of intellect, fire of determination, and unflagging faith that would sustain her in the lifetime ahead.

You Can't Rush the Lord. The same week that Pamela attended Camp Michigamme, a small group of singers from a Christian college in Iowa had come to camp to provide special inspiration in song. The double doors to the Chapel on the Hill stood open and their joyful voices reverberated in the pines.

As they sang, the presence of the Lord grew ever more palpable. The campers – boys and girls – clapped, celebrated, and began crying and hugging one another as they felt the touch of the Spirit. Many were kneeling before an altar call was even offered.

I believed in the Lord, but despite the power of the music, I sat stiffly in my pew, staring at a picture of the gentle Jesus over the altar. I asked Jesus to give me the experience others around me were having. But the more the singers and campers rejoiced, the more alienated I felt. Surely there must be something wrong with me. Was my faith that weak?

I slipped out of the chapel, the music growing fainter as I walked restlessly about the grounds, going nowhere in particular. It was nearly dark and well past what should have been the end of Bill's workday, but there he was, walking toward me on the pathway between the chapel and cabins.

"Something is bothering you, isn't it Jan?" he queried in that ever gentle manner. "You look lost. Do you want to talk?"

He had opened the floodgates and the feelings poured out.

"I want to feel like the others do," I said. "I need to know, really know, that Jesus has come into my heart, not just say the prayers even though I mean them with all my heart. Why doesn't it happen for me, Bill?"

He laid his hand lightly on my shoulder. His words were few but firm.

"You can't rush the Lord, my friend. He will know when the time is right. He will know."

Then he took my hands and enfolded them in his as I cried. He said

Bill Hampton with the author, 1995

nothing for a very long time and didn't need to. I could feel Jesus' love flowing through the warmth of those strong, calloused hands.

Michigamme and Beyond. Bill and I kept in touch over the years as I know he did with many of the people who had been a part of Michigamme. His counsel was always wise and unfailing.

Once, after I had written to him about my hope that I might survive the unrelenting criticisms of a very difficult boss, he responded, "...God will direct you in the use of your talents... Don't get impatient. All in due time."

Feeling defeated and discouraged, I left the position I loved after finally succumbing to the stress. Bill did not give up on me but wrote, "... we must have faith in the Master plan, that all things work for good for those who trust in Him. Keep the faith." Each time I sought comfort and encouragement, he offered it without reserve. "...there is something better awaiting you. You'll see!"

Chapel on the Hill in the winter (background)
Photo: Michigamme Methodist Institute

Bill retired in 1987, devoting himself to the care of his wife, Berenice, and their little house on a hill in Champion. While his career was winding down, mine was just gearing up. My husband and I had bought a home. Our trips back to my hometown in the Upper Peninsula were farther between, much less trekking as far north as Champion and Michigamme.

Still, we managed to visit Bill and Berenice four times over the years, each time being welcomed with abundant love and grace. It was during those visits, uncomplicated by the demands of campers and camp repairs, that I learned more about this kindly man.

Bill Hampton was born September 20, 1906, in Negaunee, Michigan, "... just one thousand feet from where iron ore was discovered in the Lake Superior region in 1845 by William Burke," he noted with a certain delight. The oldest of seven, Bill was born at home, as were all children in those days. His father was a miner who went to work in the dank, darkness of the bowels of the earth at the age of fifteen.

Like most children at the turn of the century, Bill walked to school which for him was one mile. While some old folks regale in exaggerated accounts of how rough it was back "when I was your age," exaggeration wasn't necessary for Bill. In northern Upper Michigan near Lake Superior with its vicious winter winds, there were many weeks of sub-zero temperatures and icy blizzards that, like the line from a famous poem by Alaskan poet, Robert Service, "Stabbed like a driven nail."

"Roads were not plowed in the winter," Bill explained. "They were kept open by the delivery sleighs of the local stores. In stormy weather we went to school on skis. There were no such things as 'snow days' that allowed us to stay home. Everyone, kids and teachers alike, lived within walking distance."

Bill was the role model for his younger siblings, though, with that trademark soft smile, he called himself, "the black sheep of the family."

"I went to the Episcopal Church with my grandma. The rest of the family was Methodist. I'm not even sure anymore why she decided to take me," he said, rubbing a finger thoughtfully across his lips. "As children, values were impressed on us to go to Sunday School. Sunday was our family day." His affirmative nod lends emphasis to the words.

"There was lots of love. Each one of us was taught to pray as soon as we could talk. We would kneel and say our prayers before getting in to bed each night. God was very real to us." Bill's voice was as steady as it could be for a man in his late eighties whose health was failing but whose faith was not.

"Our father didn't smoke, drink, or swear and was very patient and loving. Our mother was a perfect mate for him. They were examples of how loving and caring Christians should live. We were taught to share and care. It is a family trait."

Bill did not talk about sharing and caring to heap credit on himself. Quite the contrary. His statement was made simply to affirm a value that he respected and held dear throughout a lifetime.

"My mother was always there for us. One time when I was just a young boy, my brother and I were going to take the money we'd saved and buy ourselves new hats. We walked to the store and picked out the hats we liked. The only problem was that I had to stuff tissue paper inside the band of mine to hold it on my head and his was so small he had to be careful or it would fall off."

He paused, remembering how he and his brother looked as they paraded home.

"We were so proud of our new purchases, but my mother took one look at us and said, 'Take 'em back and this time when you go, take your heads with you!'"

After graduating from high school, a feat accomplished by all seven Hampton children at a time when it was common for teens to quit to take outside jobs or to work on the family farm, Bill went to work at the mines.

He was lucky not to be assigned to work inside the heavy, ore dust-fouled air of the mines where many men acquired life-limiting silicosis. Instead, he was put on the steam shovel crew which loaded iron ore into railroad cars to be transported to the ore docks at Marquette. From there, it was transferred to boats, to be shipped to the steel mills.

Bill worked the mine job from 1925 to 1932 with a good share of his earnings going to help his family so that his four younger brothers and two sisters could stay in school. In the late 1920s he began dating a local girl, but it was her sister, Lillian, who eventually won his heart. He and Lillian were married in 1929 and remained in Negaunee.

"I remember one Thanksgiving... I was already married by that time and my brother and I were figuring on going hunting the same as we always had. Our wives had told us, 'No' but we had it set in our heads to go anyway."

He leaned back in his chair, his cheeks taking on a pink, Santa-like glow, "Ah, but that was before my mother found out!"

He began laughing so hard he could hardly continue.

"Mother says, 'What's this I hear? You're NOT going hunting!'" He leaned forward and punctuated the air with a pointed finger. "We didn't either!"

In 1932, during the Great Depression, the mines closed. Bill worked at odd jobs for a time until in March of 1936, when along with thousands of others, hungry, and hungry for work, he competed for one of the few job openings for railway mail clerks. A three-hour examination tested speed, accuracy, mental recall, the ability to follow instructions, and general knowledge.

Good parenting, a high school education, and a willingness to work paid off. He did so well on the exam that in July he was ordered to report for duty at the Federal Building in St. Paul, Minnesota. There, he was assigned to work at the Post Office terminal, later transferring to work on the railroad itself, filling in for regular clerks who were on vacation or sick leave. He began riding the Soo Line, covering runs in the Upper Peninsula, Wisconsin, and Minnesota. Bill rode trains named the South Shore, the NorthWestern, the Wisconsin, and the Minnesota. His assignments took him as far west as Thief River Falls, Minnesota; north to Fort Frances, Ontario; south to Chicago, Illinois; and east to Mackinaw City, Michigan.

While the train rolled along he sorted, processed, and readied the mail for each stopping point. It was a good job except for the fact that it meant being gone from home an entire week at a time, although a week on the rails was equalled by a week at home.

Bill and Lillian moved to St. Paul in 1939 and lived there for two years before returning to Michigan. After a short time in both Marquette and Negaunee, they settled in Champion where he was assigned to the train running between Champion and Calumet. At last, Bill was able to work during the day and be home at night, something that was very important to him because the Hampton family was growing. Three children – Lorraine, William, and Virginia – completed the family circle.

Bill's work with the Postal Service railroad delivery continued until 1967.

"When the trains stopped running so did I," he says. "I retired. I didn't have to retire, but I would have had to move because they wanted me to transfer to Milwaukee, Wisconsin, which would have cost me money in the long run. Expenses to live there would have been greater, but the pay would have stayed the same."

The Postal Service's loss was Camp Michigamme's gain. Bill had volunteered as a camp counselor there for four consecutive summers, working with junior high and elementary school-age children. So, when the position of camp manager became available in 1968, he was an ideal candidate. His grasp of the challenges faced by counselors, his deep faith, and his ability to work well with counselors, staff, children, and parents, made him the natural choice.

"A week of counseling leaves a person spiritually on Cloud Nine but physically exhausted," he said, knowing how well I understood.

The spiritual rewards outweighed the physical drawbacks. "Michigamme was a labor of love from the start. I would have done that for nothing," he says, with a chuckle.

His work to prepare for the summer onslaught of thundering, energetic feet began in April, and the work consumed his days and nights until the buildings were closed for the winter by late October. Most of what he earned as camp manager he donated back to the camp in the form of anonymous scholarships, so that needy children could spend a week at camp. Many children who delighted in his hugs and unflagging encouragement never knew that he was the person who had made their stay possible.

Meanwhile, he and Lillian lived a simple life five miles from the campground. At the age of eighty-nine he was still quietly providing scholarships.

"I was sixty-one and in good health when I assumed the responsibilities of camp manager. I remained in good physical condition, retiring at eighty-one, still hale and hearty! I theorize it was the contact with the kids. I believe I un-aged three months each summer." His eyes sparkle. "With so much exuberance of youth permeating the atmosphere, I must have assimilated some of it by osmosis. There sure is a lot of energy in a camp full of kids!"

The summer before he retired, Bill and a young grandson, scaled tall ladders to update the maintenance on the entire Chapel on the Hill.

"We talk about the trouble with kids these days, but I have seen and heard their testimonies on Hilltop and in the Chapel on the Hill," he says quietly. His deeply-held confidence in the ability of the human spirit to overcome its weaker side is evident in his voice.

"I remember a group of singers who came one year from Dallas, Texas. One night while they were there, the Northern Lights filled the sky. They'd never seen anything like it. I told them that I'd asked God to do that for them so they could see the lights. I think they believed me!" He flashes an impish grin.

Bill lost his teenage son to leukemia. Lillian died in 1970, and a short time after that, his sister-in-law's husband passed away.

After so many good years of love and companionship, the deaths left voids in the lives of Bill and his sister-in-law, Berenice. The two found companionship with one another, were married, and brought together their families, including the church camp family.

"The families who come to camp every year are part of my extended family," he said happily. "God has blessed me richly. How fortunate I have been."

A lifetime of service to others, and of helping young people searching to make their way in the world, convinced Bill Hampton of the three most important values he believed a person can have. He offered them without hesitation or doubt. "… faith, responsibility, and honesty. Without those, a person is not living as he should."

Bill embodied those values and when, shortly before his ninety-first birthday, he left this life to go on to a higher calling, he carried them into his next tour of duty.

The Chapel on the Hill has been fittingly renamed Hampton Chapel. Its solid timbers are like the solid tenor of his faith, its simplicity is the unpretentiousness of his way of being in the world, and its inviting sanctuary is his welcoming hug.

There are people who come and go from our lives leaving no more lasting impression than a whisper on the wind. But there are others whose imprint lasts forever. Bill Hampton was one such person.

A Counselor's Prayer

I came alone
To this well-trodden place atop the hill
Where a birch cross stands framed against fully greened trees
and a summer sky of blue

High above me
Branches blow in the mid-morning breeze
A bird sings
A bee buzzes
No human sound is heard
but the rhythm of my own breathing

I feel at peace here
And closer to God than ever before

The sun warms the cross and my bowed head

I pray for a patient heart
A kindly voice
An understanding way
As I seek to find myself in helping others
I pray that
I can instill in the hearts
of these youth
A sense of appreciation and grateful respect
For others and for
Our Creator.

Amen

Jan Corey
1973

Adopted Grandmas and Gifts of Love

A faded dress, a baby quilt, a wedding ring, a dogwood tree.

"My grandmother was such a wonderful lady," my friend, Angie, said wistfully as we visited over tea. "I wish she were still here."

Angie's grandmother had been everything warm and wonderful the word brings to mind – a patient listener, cheerleader, cookie-baker, hug-giver.

"You can't ever quite replace her, but you could adopt," I suggested.

"Do what?" she replied, scrunching her eyebrows.

"You could find someone who would make a good grandmother and adopt her."

I poured more tea and as the morning sun tiptoed across the room, I told Angie about my adopted grandmothers.

Adopting a grandmother came easily because I had not had the privilege of having a close relationship with my natural grandmothers. Grandma Corey had passed away before I was born, and Grandma Palmer had many health problems. By the time I was old enough to spend the night with her as my sisters once had (when they would get themselves in trouble for rummaging through her steamer trunk in the attic), she no longer tolerated having children around for more than a brief visit.

Had I consciously set out to find a grandma-like figure to fill the void?

No matter. Each of the four ladies who have been a part of my adult life has, through her own blend of spirituality, touch of eccentricity, and time-tested wisdom, brought clarity to my view of life.

I was eleven and **Monica** was in her late seventies when I adopted her. She and her husband, Joseph, barely eked out a living on a tiny scrap of land near the Upper Michigan farm where I was raised in the 1950s

Monica Mikuchonis

and 1960s. Polish was their first language, English a distant second. They had been born in Poland in 1886 and like so many other immigrants sought freedom, opportunity, and a better life in the United States.

One afternoon when I was out riding my pony on the gravel roads that connected country farms, I found a forlorn and hungry-looking cat that was eager to nestle against my shoulder as I headed for the nearest farm.

"Yah, is our gat," Monica said tearfully, when she answered my tap on their door, the tabby cat cradled in her arms.

Her braided, wispy white hair was coiled at the nape of her neck. She and Joseph wore faded, many-times-mended clothing. He quickly hobbled out to a few gnarly old apple trees behind the house and picked a basket of the best apples he could find.

"Is for you," he said, the basket cupped between arthritic hands stained by hard work. "Is for you."

After that, when I went riding, I often chose to head west to the Mikuchonis farm to visit with Monica and Joseph. Their faces lit up on seeing me and made me feel ever so important. It mattered little that we communicated more with smiles than with words.

My mother, always generous with the bounty of her garden, often sent along a bouquet of flowers or a basket of vegetables which the couple accepted with humility, tears coming easily to their old eyes. They had little. They worked hard.

Rarely did I find them in the beaten old farmhouse. More often they were bent over in their potato field, hoeing, weeding, and watering. But they worked as a team and lived with simple gratitude. When they looked at one another, deep respect shone in their eyes.

Faith was keenly important to Monica and Joseph.

"You have belief in Got?" they asked one day as the pony buried his face in long grass along their driveway and I downed a glass of cold, clear water that Joseph pumped for me from the well in the yard.

"Yes, I believe…"

"Is goot. He is our Father." They nodded enthusiastically. "Yah, is goot."

After Joseph's death in 1968, Monica closed off most of the drafty, aging farmhouse. Life centered around the old woodstove in the center of the sparsely-furnished living room. The stove was her source of heat and the place where she also sometimes prepared what little she cooked, now that she had no one to cook for but herself. Fried potatoes, an egg, soups, and beans, were often what I saw when she invited me in to visit with her.

Life without Joseph was barely life, but what little she had, she shared with joy. "This, I get from Old Countra," she would say, pressing a lovely little tin of hard candy into my hand that family so far away had mailed to her. "Got is goot to me. I be goot to you!"

I continued to visit Monica, especially after my parents sold our farm and moved closer to town, less than a mile from the Mikuchonis farm. The first time I visited after getting my driver's license, it amazed her that a woman could drive a car. This was something she had never learned to do or perhaps had never thought she should do. She found it fascinating to peer through the windows at all the gadgets, buttons, and numbers on the dashboard.

Before I left home to attend college in the fall of 1971, she hugged me as if I might never return, took my hands in hers, the fingers gnarled from arthritis and years of work, and said, "Learn much. Come home, teach Monica."

Monica was cautiously happy when, soon after graduating from college four years later, I became engaged. "Is he goot man?" she asked warily. "He work? He belief in Got?"

She led me to a long-unused back bedroom, the bedroom she had shared with Joseph and likely had never slept in again when he was no longer beside her. She opened a closet and pushed back a dusty yellowed sheet draped over the clothes rack to reveal a few tired cotton dresses. Carefully she studied them, perhaps lost for a moment in the memories they evoked of happier times when she and Joseph were young.

Had Monica ever danced? What had she looked like as a bride? Might Joseph have chosen any of these dresses for her when she was young, her waist was slender, and a lifetime seemed to stretch endlessly ahead of them?

After a moment of fondly running her hands over each one, she proudly selected the nicest of them, held it up to me and said, "This be goot dress, wear for your man Sundays. Yah?"

We hugged. As I left with the neatly-folded dress in hand, her old eyes sparkled, "You tell your man take goot care of you. Monica say so!"

Monica Mikuchonis died in 1977, less than a year after I was married. The apple orchard and the old shingled farmhouse are gone, replaced by shrubbery and a vinyl-sided modular dwelling. Yet, I can see her there across the years, working side by side with her "man."

Shared faith, loyalty, and respect are the stuff of which good marriages are made. Monica showed me that.

Sara Harrod

Sara came into my life mid-way through my college years. I needed an inexpensive place to live near campus for a couple of months in the summer while I attended summer school and worked part-time at the college library. She was ninety-nine, a wisp of a woman, living alone in a wonderful old home just a stone's throw from campus, with an inviting wooden swing on the front porch. Her husband and two sons had been dead for several years.

To supplement her limited income, Sara rented upstairs rooms to working men from the community or to male college students. It was only reluctantly, on the advice of her niece that she consented to give a female renter a try. She didn't much like women, perhaps from all the years of being the only woman around the house. Her niece warned me to expect a chilly reception, but not to take it personally.

"It would be good for her not to be alone anymore, and I think she'd be safer at her age having a woman in the house than a man," her niece had said. Sara had been very matter-of-fact and curt as she informed me that I could have a bedroom with kitchen privileges for ten dollars a week.

"The last college students I agreed to rent a room to," she said in as stern a voice as age could muster, "seemed like two very nice young men. But they tried to tell me that what they were carrying up to their rooms were tomato plants."

She folded her arms like a headmistress about to get out the willow switch. "I told them I was no fool. I knew that plant was mary-ju-ana and they had better move right back out!"

Her eyes were burning a hole right through me. I knew what the next question would be.

"Do you have any of that mary-ju-ana?"

"No, Mrs. Harrod," I told her. "I have never used it and I don't intend to. If you rent to me you are welcome to come into my room any time you want to. You don't have to worry."

She was visibly relieved.

"All right then," she said. "You may rent a room. But don't be noisy with that young people's music."

Like Monica, Sara had known a life of hard work, the last twenty of it on her own. She was exceptionally orderly and regimented, insistent that everything in her kitchen be kept exactly as she had it arranged. I suppose her precision was as much because her eyesight was failing as because she had a right to have a place for everything and everything in its place. I was careful to maintain that orderliness and was mindful of her precise routine. If it meant waiting in my room listening to the growling of my own stomach, I waited, until I was absolutely certain she was finished in the kitchen for the night. Then I tiptoed downstairs, directly past the tiny sitting room that had become her bedroom. She rarely attempted to climb the steep winding stairs to the second floor, but did now and then, just to be sure everything upstairs was being maintained to her satisfaction.

As we became better acquainted, Sara invited me to eat with her and soon, dining together was a nightly routine. I had little money, she had little company. Our fare was simple but sufficient. In late May and early June when the asparagus was in season, I scuttled out of town on my bicycle after work and classes, to search along country roads for wild asparagus. I got as much pleasure out of watching her savor its tender, flavorful tips as I am sure my own mother must have when she gave those to her family, while insisting that the tough stems were really her favorite part.

Never before and never since the time spent with Sara, have I eaten so much French toast, sliced cucumbers, and fruit cocktail. But it was over those simple suppers that I learned to eat slowly and to practice patience as she shared with me the stories of her life and the hardships she had endured.

She told me about the boarder back in the 1930s who became seriously ill and had asked to be allowed to die in his room in her home. He made her promise that at the moment of his death she was to put her full weight on his contorted legs so that no cuts would have to be made or bones broken to make his body lie properly in the casket. She had honored his request.

The same year that she tended to the dying boarder, she herself was very ill from what was then called catarrh of the bowels, a severe inflammation that left her unable to eat solid food. She survived on buttermilk and burnt toast for six long months, tasting her first spoon of mashed potatoes at Christmas.

Night after night we lingered over our supper at her tiny kitchen table or in her little sitting room as I grew to love her and she to love me.

Sara's faith was as orderly as her kitchen. Every Sunday she put on the same black dress, white hose, and black pumps, rocked gently in the same rocking chair, and dutifully studied her Bible. She did no work nor did she cook on Sunday. Even her quilting waited until Monday. Sara had made dozens of quilts over the years for brand new babies and road-weary friends confined to nursing homes. To get a quilt from Sara Harrod was to be considered someone special, and during one of our long evening chats while she pieced blocks, she reached down beside her rocking chair and tenderly lifted two soft patchwork baby quilts from the top of her pile of fabric.

"These are for you and for the babies you will have some day," she said in her quavery voice, softened by a tiny, joyful smile.

Sara's bedtime ritual was announced by the distinctive scent of camphor that drifted up the stairs at the same time every evening. Her doctor had warned when she was in her fifties, that she had a bad heart. So bad, in fact, that before she left his office he had advised, "You'd best go home and get your affairs in order."

Sara made a stop on the way home that day to purchase a bottle of camphorated oil and a sack of sugar. As her mother before her, that very evening she began using camphor to remedy her heart problem. Despite the warning on the label that camphor was "for external use only," she swallowed a drop of the strong oil in a spoon of sugar, then rubbed the pure oil on her chest.

Whether the camphor served genuine medicinal purposes beyond its psychological benefit remains a question that needs no answer. She was convinced and that was all that mattered.

I avoided Sara when I wasn't feeling well, especially if I had a cold. Unselfishly, I didn't want her to catch anything at her advanced age and delicate condition. But there were also purely selfish reasons. I didn't want to submit to her home remedies, of which camphor was the least troublesome.

"You need a good, hot-boiled onion poultice for your chest," she'd insist, determined to march right to the kitchen and start peeling onions if she so much as detected a sniffle. "We'll put a poultice on your chest and then you've got to drink all the hot onion broth you can stand."

"Thanks but no thanks," I vigorously protested while backing away, though I suspected Sara was right about the camphor and the onions and a good many other things.

For Sara's one hundredth birthday she was to be feted with a fine party and honored as the oldest living Rebekah in the state of Michigan. She had joined the Rebekah Lodge at the age of eighteen, in March of 1892, and was still a member eighty-two years later.

But when she learned that Lodge members and the community were going to have a party for her, she was distraught. She wanted something special to wear for the occasion other than her black church dress. As the little whisper of a woman stood before her closet fumbling through the dresses, it was apparent that everything was either far too big, long-since out-of-style, or just not quite right for such a momentous occasion.

I shared Sara's plight as I spoke on the telephone one evening with my mother more than five hundred miles away.

Mom quickly set about to design and sew to Sara's unique size and specifications, a lovely lavender dress that fit her beautifully. The centenarian was the picture of elegance at her grand party.

Sara was one hundred and one years old when she was forced to leave her home after breaking a hip. She spent her remaining two years in a local nursing home where we continued our friendship and where she insisted on always looking her best and greeting her visitors with grace and dignity. Her life was a testimony to the peace and satisfaction to be found in obedient, orderly, and purposeful living.

Sadie Seales

"Granmaw" Sadie was near eighty and lived with her son-in-law just up the road from my husband and me after we were married in 1976. Her son-in-law, "Dunc," was in the early stages of Alzheimer's but still managed to live at home under her anxious eye. Sadie's daughter, who suffered from multiple sclerosis, had been in a nursing home for many years.

Other family members looked in on Granmaw and Dunc periodically, but my husband or I saw them every day. We had an agreement, that in exchange for their allowing us to use the tumble-down old barn on their property so I could keep a horse, we would help out with their needs. When one of us came to tend the horse morning and night, we stopped in to check on them.

It was an ideal arrangement for everyone. My husband or I drove them to town for groceries, brought them home-cooked meals and flowers from our garden, helped with little projects around the house, or just visited. It wasn't so much what we did, it was that they could be reassured that someone was taking note of their well-being.

Sadie's life had been worse than hard. It had been traumatic. After the death of her husband when she was little more than a newlywed, scheming individuals had her declared mentally incompetent, institutionalized her, and seized the property left to her by her husband. Sadie was not mentally incompetent, she was simply illiterate and therefore unable to defend herself to the legal system. As a result, she had remained confined until others learned of her plight and gained her freedom.

In spite of, or perhaps because of her painful past, Sadie found delight in just about everything.

"Pshaw, oh pshaw," was her favorite commentary. She wore a gummy smile that beamed, even when in my feeble attempts to be her beautician, I cut her hair too short or gave her perms that frizzled. She was as exuberant as a child each time she would enjoy a good soak in our bathtub followed by a pedicure and manicure. Her toenails were a challenge to trim, not so much because they were crooked and thick, but because her waddy little feet were ticklish. The moment my hand touched her foot to do the trimming, she'd start to twitch and wiggle like a bunny, giggling the entire time.

"Oh pshaw! You girl!" she'd say while her foot bounced this way and that. To Sadie, these ordinary events could not have been more celebrated if they'd been given at a posh salon rather than in my dowdy living room in an old country schoolhouse-turned-apartment.

Never once in the seven or so years we were buddies did Granmaw Sadie ever call me by my given name. I was always "Girl," but she spoke it with affection. "Oh you Girl!"

Sometimes when I'd happen to be near a window or working in my yard I'd see little Granmaw Sadie and her burly son-in-law hiking down the road on their way to or from town about five miles away. When he could no longer remember the way, Granmaw took the lead, intent on getting to their favorite watering hole for a beer. They never asked to be driven, but everyone in the neighborhood knew Granmaw and Dunc, so rarely did they have to walk the entire stretch, though they would have for a beer.

Granmaw loved beer, pouring it so quickly, warm or cold, that it would form a big head of foam that she would suck off the top of the glass with an exaggerated, "Ooossssh....ahhhh" made quite dramatic by her complete lack of teeth. And when she didn't have beer she kept a little bottle of alcohol-laced cough syrup in the cupboard for an occasional nip. If I happened to be there when she reached in the cupboard for whatever brand was on hand, she'd rub her hand across her throat, swallow hard, cough ever so unconvincingly, saying "Ahem... ahem... I've got a sore throat."

Eventually Dunc's Alzheimer's worsened to the point that he could no longer be left at home with only an elderly mother-in-law to look after him. He was placed in foster care and not long after that Sadie's family, not wanting her to be alone on the farm, decided to move her to a lovely group foster care home.

The night before Sadie was to leave the farm, I found her in her bedroom among clothes strewn across the bed. She was hunched over a scarred old wooden jewelry box, toying with a few pieces of dime store jewelry.

"Is there something I can help you with Granmaw?" I asked sitting beside her on the thread-bare yellow spread. What must she be thinking and feeling as this major change was about to occur in her life?

"Oh Girl," she said softly, "Granmaw don't have much to pack." There was no hiding that she had mixed emotions about leaving the only home she'd known for many years to move into a strange setting. I felt relief that she would be looked after, but loss, too, that I would not be able to see her every day and be met with that gummy smile and "Oh Girl!"

She fumbled about in the wooden box until, under some faded handkerchiefs, she found a wide gold wedding band etched with a floral design and tiny eyelets. "I want you to have this," she said, reaching for my hand.

"I can't Granmaw," I told her, pressing the wedding band back into her hand. "I'm not family."

Her eyes narrowed, not in anger but in conviction as she put the band back into my hand, folded my fingers over it, and said, "You are more family to me than anybody and what they don't know won't hurt 'em!" She was insistent.

I gave her a hug, overwhelmed by her gift but more by her words.

"Oh pshaw," she chortled when she saw my tears. "Pshaw."

Granmaw took a fast liking to the foster care home and was content where she had three good meals, a bedtime snack, and constant attention. She was a favorite of the staff.

My parents had met Granmaw Sadie on their visits to Lower Michigan and I kept them informed of what was going on in her life as circumstances changed. Once Granmaw was settled into her new surroundings, my mother crocheted a lovely lap robe to keep Sadie's shoulders or knees warm when she sat in the living room watching television and waiting for visitors. Sadie was rarely without it.

One afternoon in response to a compelling inner nudge, I made a special trip to visit Granmaw Sadie. We knew she had been failing but something said, *Go now.*

I found her near death. One of the aides was at her side. I held her hand and talked to her for a few moments as she lay with her eyes closed. She relaxed visibly when she heard my voice and smiled a weak gummy smile.

Half an hour later, Granmaw was gone.

Life can hand us many injustices but we can choose to be imprisoned by them or to move on. When I need to remind myself not to relive old wrongs, I think of Granmaw Sadie and the hardships she overcame to find joy in the absolute simplicity of her life. "Oh pshaw," I hear her say. "You Girl!"

Irene literally showed up at my door. She was seventy-four, I was twenty-nine. She was good friends with an elderly neighbor who was no longer able to drive and had volunteered, this glorious day in May, to bring him to our house so he could give my husband and me fresh asparagus from his yard. We had only lived in the neighborhood a short time.

Irene asked questions about anything and everything as we gave her and "Billy D" a tour of our yard with its vegetable and flower gardens. Her Boston terriers, Heidi and Cindi, raced wildly back and forth across the lawn, delighting in country freedom.

At first I thought I might not take a liking to this woman who asked so many questions and offered unsolicited advice. But wonderfully enough, our mutual eccentricities made us fast friends. Before long I nicknamed her "Reeni" and she called me "Dolly." In the sixteen years to follow, we would discover that we both saved too many old letters, newspaper clippings, and bits of writings, until the paper clutter made us nervous. We had too many books we still hoped to read and too many craft projects still on the maybe-someday list. We loved to feed wild birds and talk to the little animals as if they were family. We were both drawn over and over to certain Bible passages and were happiest when we could be out-of-doors. We loved old hats, browsing in antique shops, and doing silly spontaneous things just because they were there to be done. Most of all, we staunchly agreed, life without a dog is hardly life at all.

There was rarely a conversation when we visited one another's homes or spoke on the phone that she didn't say, "Dolly, you are my light in a dark place." Her own daughter and granddaughter rarely visited. She missed them terribly.

In serious moments Reeni dispensed sound advice about the ways of the world, always weaving references to biblical teaching into her words. Her own Bible was well underlined and annotated with personal observations penned carefully in the margins.

"Honor your father and mother, that your days may be long upon the land," (Exodus 20:12) she often reminded me. She knew the importance of the verse. Reeni had cared for both of her parents through their long illnesses. Her love and loyalty were so great that, after her young husband died, she married a much older man whom she didn't love because she knew he would help her take care of her mother who was dying of "female cancer."

"My sweet angel mom," Reeni would say wistfully, "someday I will see my sweet angel mom again."

After Billy D was moved a couple of hundred miles away to a foster home in Ohio near his daughters, my husband and I took Reeni to visit him two or three times a year. She and I would do an injustice to old hymns that we belted out with great enthusiasm, while my tolerant husband did the driving and stifled his laughter. When mercifully our singing stopped, she would thank him for his patience and remind him that I was her "light in a dark place."

Reeni had a stubborn streak a football field long, and there were times when it seemed that every shred of what little patience I had, was tested by her latest indecision or tangent. It took forever for her to make the painful decision to have Heidi put to sleep after the terrier had suffered long and hard with a skin disease that left its hide raw and oozing, and drove the little dog frantic with itching. Visiting Reeni for more than a few minutes had become nearly impossible because of the rank odor from the old dog.

"I suppose you're going to tell me like everybody else does that you are busy and can't stay long?" she snapped one day as I leaned against the doorframe between the kitchen and backdoor, trying not to breathe through my nose.

"Reeni, I am going to tell you the truth," I said, finally unable to keep the truth from her. "People aren't staying long because of the smell from the dogs. It's awful."

Her temper flared. I was the proverbial messenger about to be shot. It took more than a day or two or three for her to acknowledge that just maybe the smell was overpowering, the dog was miserable, and that it was indeed time to do something about poor, sad Heidi. She hemmed and hawed, fretted and fussed.

When Reeni finally called one Saturday to tell me, albeit reluctantly, that she was finally ready to do what had to be done, I dropped what I was doing. Weekends were always hectic as I tried to get things done around home, but this was more important. I quickly threw an old blanket across the back seat of my car and headed for her house, hoping she wouldn't change her mind before I got there as she had before.

She had.

"I can't do it," she moaned while, to relieve the horrible itching, the poor pathetic old dog writhed in the trench it had dug in the backyard. Heidi was miserable and worn out in more ways than one.

"Reeni," I pleaded as gently as I could. "It is time. We have to do this for Heidi's sake."

Reluctantly, she let me lift Heidi into the car. With the window open, I drove to the clinic where once again she balked, demanding that I turn the car right around and take Heidi home.

This time I was the one who was so stubborn that I shocked myself. I was not at all used to speaking to my elders in a sharp tone of voice.

"Reeni, I hate this too and I don't have time to go through this again. I have better things to do on a Saturday morning than run ten miles across town for nothing! This is the second time we have been through this and if we don't do this now, don't you ever ask me to help you with this again! Period!"

I sat behind the steering wheel with a white-knuckle grip and a beady-eyed glare.

The car was completely silent, the smell from the back seat growing worse by the moment.

Reeni turned to me with a look of complete astonishment on her face as a knot grew in the pit of my stomach. Never had I spoken to her like that. She knew it and I knew it.

She feebly nodded consent and sat numbly as I hustled into the clinic and pleaded my case to the several people (and pets) ahead of us.

"Please let us go ahead of you before she changes her mind again!" I begged.

No one protested.

Reeni waited in the car, clutching Heidi's leash and a soggy hander-chief as I comforted Heidi and the vet did what had to be done. Minutes later, with Heidi wrapped in the faded blanket, Reeni and I headed home to bury her old companion behind the garage beside a patch of berry bushes she called "the back forty."

With Heidi gone, much of the odor left Reeni's house. Lingering for a visit over a cup of tea or her watered-down cranberry juice was much more pleasant. Cindi seemed well and for a long time remained good company for Irene. But then, out of the blue, the terrier began to suffer first one seizure and then another. Seeing her remaining dog in such dire straits sent Irene into a frenzy. The vet said the seizures would likely get worse. With them came bowel and bladder problems that poor Cindi could not help, but made Irene's house worse off than it had been when Heidi was alive. Irene knew it. I knew it.

Mercifully, Cindi died on her own.

"Do you think you could bury Cindi at your place?" Reeni asked. "She loved to run in your big yard and I could visit her there."

"Of course we can bury her at my place, Reeni," I said, offering to get the grave ready.

But before I could begin digging, Reeni had changed her mind. She wanted to take Cindi out to her niece's place on the other side of town and bury her there. Her niece agreed and together we dug a grave, laid Cindi in it, covered it and placed flowers on top. It was over.

Well, not quite.

A day later, my phone rang. "Dolly," Reeni began in a strained voice, "I just can't leave little Cindi out there all by herself. We've got to bring her back home and put her with Heidi."

"Dig her up?" I asked in dismay.

"She's only been there a little while. It won't hurt anything."

"I know… but are you sure?"

"I'm sure."

Exhuming a dead animal was not a chore I relished, but it was true that the dog had not even been buried twenty-four hours. It would be a nuisance job but not yet terribly offensive.

But before I could pick Reeni up to drive out to her niece's house she had changed her mind and called back.

"No, it's okay to leave Cindi there," she said. "She liked that yard. We can leave her there."

I breathed a sign of relief. It was over.

But not quite.

Two days later and several degrees warmer, Reeni was still fretting about Cindi's final resting place.

"I want to bring her home and bury her on the back forty" she insisted.

"Reeni!" I protested. "Cindi has been buried for three whole days and it is eighty degrees outside. Do you know how things are going to have changed?" My stomach was already turning at the very thought of digging up the dead dog.

"I don't care!" she wailed. "I want to bury Cindi right here at home. It won't matter to me. I can stand anything."

I called her niece who simply sighed, "That's my aunt Irene. If she wants Cindi dug up we'll do it or she'll fret forever."

But this time, before I could even take Irene to her niece's house, she had changed her mind again, and finally, to my eternal relief, it was over. Cindi could at last rest in peace. And so could I.

The episodes with the dogs were not the last examples of Reeni's stubborn streak. One winter when the ice hung heavy until limbs snapped and lines were severed, cutting off power to whole sections of the county, I begged Reeni to let us bring her to our house. Half the city of Battle Creek was out of electricity, but we were secure even if rural power went out. We had a good-sized woodstove in our basement, a fireplace upstairs, and plenty of split wood. We could stay toasty warm and make coffee and soup on the woodstove if necessary.

"No, Dolly," she said adamantly, "I know you mean well, but Reeni is staying put. I can go down in my basement and put a fire in my old woodstove. I'll be just fine."

Temperatures dropped drastically that night and I tossed and turned, thinking of that woman in her eighties, alone in an old house, huddling at the bottom of steep concrete stairs in a dank basement. Her tiny stove was barely big enough for a stick or two of wood. There was no way she could manage.

The next morning I crept my way to town over icy roads soon after daylight.

"You are coming home with me, Reeni and don't you argue!" I said authoritatively, somewhat reminiscent of a tirade in a vet clinic parking lot. Her puny little stove had barely given off enough heat to keep her warm and she had stayed awake nearly the whole night feeding the fire. She was too chilled to argue. I brought her home with me where she spent the next few days fussing and fretting until the power was restored to her neighborhood.

The children in Reeni's rundown neighborhood all knew her as Grandma Jay, short for her last name, Jaycox. They often came by to tell her all the things that are so important to children because Grandma Jay listened attentively and never let them leave without two or three cookies clenched in grubby hands. She would sit adoringly with them on her back porch while they chewed and chattered.

Sometimes in the winter she swapped cookies for snowmen, praising the kids as they rolled and packed balls and set them on top of one another. She'd come up with an old hat or a carrot nose, give her frozen friend a name, and talk to him every morning while she fixed breakfast until he was subjected to a sunny day diet plan.

One winter during perfect snowman weather, when I was fighting the flu, I mentioned to my mother that Reeni was feeling badly because she didn't have a frozen friend to keep vigil in her backyard. My parents by this time had moved to Battle Creek and knew Reeni quite well from all the times she was included in our family doings. Despite my mother's own age and arthritis, she quietly got into her car, drove to Irene's and surreptitiously built a snow-man while Reeni napped, completely unaware that a woman with hair as white as the snow she packed into place, was at work in her backyard. Reeni was ecstatic when she awoke to find a handsome new buddy standing at attention near her door.

Irene Jaycox and friend

For my forty-second birthday, Reeni joyfully presented me with a pink dogwood tree. "To remember me by when I'm gone, Dolly," she said, as we had a blessing of the tree in my yard. She had begun to speak more often and more longingly of the day when she would join her "sweet angel mom in heaven." The anticipation was building. True to the biblical edict, she had honored her father and mother and her own days had been long on the earth, but she was now ready for them to draw to a close.

A stroke when she was eighty-seven made it difficult for Irene to continue to live alone at home, but still my friend was a ready supply of what I dubbed, "Reeni-isms." By her own admission she would say with the flair of a comedienne, "Dolly, my face looks like ten miles of bad roads," or, "My face has more lines than the phone company." Ask how well she'd slept the night and she'd quip, "When I got up this morning my eyes looked like two burned holes in a blanket." She never ended a visit without the words, "You are still my light in a dark place."

Reeni willingly moved to the assisted-living section of a progressive care home where she lived contentedly for a year before another stroke necessitated a move to the full nursing care floor and a third took away her ability to walk and to be understood. It was terribly frustrating for her to not be able to say what she wanted to say. She tried, but all that came forth was babble, punctuated by smiles and an intense gaze that said that what she was trying to get across mattered a great deal.

On one of our last visits, she studied my face a long time as I sat beside her, then, without so much as a stutter, said softly and clearly, "You are still my light in a dark place."

I wept.

It was only a short time later, just past her ninetieth birthday, that she slipped away, to be with her angel mom, leaving me to remember the joy to be found in our mutual eccentricities and friendship across the ages.

A faded cotton dress, a baby quilt, a wedding ring, a dogwood tree – I have gifts by which to remember each of my adopted grandmothers. But these things, precious as they are, are not what matters. What matters is the bond of love I was privileged to share with the people who gave them.

But I might have overlooked an even greater love had I not written

Mom

of these dear friends all these years later. There are also the baskets of vegetables, a lovely lavender dress, a warm lap robe, a secret snowman and dozens of other kind things that my own mother did for these adopted grandmas because of her love for me and her generosity to others.

There have been many gifts, but the greatest of these is my mother's love.

Am I Dying?

She shook her head from side to side after each question, the tears still wetting her face as she began to take short, gasping breaths.

In the years after my sisters and I left Michigan's Upper Peninsula, first to attend college, then to marry and make our homes in other parts of the state and country, homecomings were rare and extra special.

We surprised our parents one summer by conspiring to show up on their doorstep – all five of us – together. Some of the grand-kids came along, making it a real reunion. The kids giggled and ran through the sprinkler, waded in the pond behind the house, and climbed the big hill that overlooked the little city of Stephenson. We helped Mom and Dad with their garden, which was the envy of many folks in the area who sometimes drove by just to admire "the Corey place."

A meal with Mom and Dad was a feast – a bounty of fresh wholesome food – strawberries, raspberries, asparagus, carrots, peas, and homemade apple pies made with apples from their own trees. Even the kids were eating vegetables they would have ignored at their own homes! Our family togetherness around the table was something right out of a painting by Norman Rockwell.

After supper one evening, Dad was telling the kids another of his many stories about growing up in the early 1900s on the family farm just a few miles away. The kids seemed to never get enough of Grandpa's stories and the telling and retelling of them brought him great satisfaction. He could relive precious moments and if the stories had become ever so slightly embellished over time, who cared?

Just around the corner from where Dad and the kids were gathered in the living room, Mom, a couple of my sisters, and I were working in the kitchen, wiping dishes and putting things away, whispering quietly.

I felt a tap on my arm and looked down to find Corina, my sister Lois' daughter, looking up at me, her eyes wide with fear. "Aunt Jan," she said, "can you come with me?" She was perhaps nine or ten, a sweet round-faced girl with a bubbly laugh. She tugged anxiously at my arm. "Since my mom isn't here right now, can I tell you something?"

It was obvious from the way she clung to my sleeve and her eyes darted about to see who might be listening, that whatever she needed to say she didn't want anyone else to hear. We tiptoed to a bedroom at

the back of the house and she motioned for me to sit beside her on the bed. She stared at her feet and fussed with her hands as if afraid to speak.

I waited. Something was bothering her terribly. What could possibly be wrong? I slipped my arm around her shoulder.

Mark, Paul, Elizabeth, Jennifer, Greg and Corina

"Corina," I encouraged, "what's wrong?"

Still she stared at her bare feet, then after a long while looked up at me, tears filling her eyes and spilling down her delicate flawless cheeks.

"Aunt Jan, I... I think I'm dying," she said, her voice quivering. She bit her lower lip and let out a gasp, clutching her stomach.

Dying?

This was not at all what I had expected to hear.

"Dying? What makes you think you are dying?" I asked, trying not to appear at all alarmed and add to her fear. "Does your stomach hurt? Does your head hurt? Do you feel sick?"

She shook her head from side to side after each question, the tears still wetting her face as she began to take short, gasping breaths.

I laid my palm to her forehead and to her pink cheeks. She showed no sign of fever.

"Tell me what's wrong that you think you are dying," I prodded, gently drawing her closer to me.

"I... I..." she clenched and unclenched her hands. "I went to the bathroom a little while ago and it was all blood," she said in a rush. "I am bleeding to death!"

"Blood? You saw blood?" I asked, wanting to make certain I had heard her correctly.

She was fighting tears as she nodded, "Yes."

"It was bright red? Was there a lot of it?"

Again she nodded. She could barely contain herself and began to tremble. Each time she answered, "Yes," it was as if she'd been given just that much more confirmation that death was imminent.

"How long has this been going on?"

"Just... just today," she sobbed in broken gasps.

I sat beside her for a bit, rubbing her back as she trembled, searching my mind for the right thing to do.

What in the world could possibly have happened? She had played happily, she'd laughed and had run through the sprinkler. She hadn't injured herself, at least not that she had said anything to anyone about. She had shown absolutely no signs of illness. She had eaten very well.

Eaten....

"Corina, did you, by any chance, have some of Grandma's cooked beets for lunch yesterday?" I asked.

She gazed up at me, her eyes growing wide.

"Uh huh," she said, almost afraid to admit that she had eaten them. Now she knew she was going to die. There was something wrong with the sweet garden beets she had enjoyed so much!

"I ate lots of 'em," she confessed, barely in a whisper.

Relief washed over me and I began to smile.

She stared at me in disbelief. She was dying and Aunt Jan was smiling?

"You're not dying," I grinned. "It's the beets!"

She thought for a moment, peering at me with innocent confusion. Then, all at once she blushed, giggled, hugged me hard, and bounced out the door, happy with her new lease on life and a newfound appreciation for the magic of Grandma's garden.

A Love Everlasting

*The golden light from a nearby lamp cast a peaceful glow across her face.
As his hand rested on her hair he turned, looked up at me and whispered ever
so softly, "Isn't she beautiful?"*

The first time I saw Jane Sherriff, she was perched on a tall stool
aboard a pontoon boat built for taking large groups on lake excursions.
She listened attentively as her husband Fred, narrated a tour of Michigan's
Gull Lake. It was August, 1985, and as the boat putta-putta'd steadily
along, Fred highlighted points of interest about the lake and the people
whose property lined its shores. Few knew the lake any better than Fred
Sherriff, or delighted more in relating its history.

"Over there are the grounds of the Kellogg Biological Station. The
large home on the hill," he said, motioning toward a tudor-style mansion,
"was once the summer residence of W. K. Kellogg, who created the cereal
company and, of course, the foundation where you all work. Mr. Kellogg
gave his property to Michigan State University and today it is a research
station responsible for much of the work done to safeguard this lake, one
of the best spring-fed lakes in the country."

Fred Sherriff had known the famous Mr. Kellogg personally, although
he himself was just a boy when the cereal magnate spent time at the lake,
not far from where Fred's family also owned property. Fred's father was a
highly successful businessman in the Battle Creek community, who, with
his business partner, had established a commercial and residential roofing
business at about the time W.K. Kellogg was experimenting with flaked
cereal. Now that Fred was at the helm of the roofing company, one might

assume that he would be caught up in self-importance. He was anything but self-important. Down to earth and sincere, Fred was just good folks. In fact, he was uncomfortable with pretense and hoopla. He laughed easily as he shared tidbits of information, sometimes reaching up to run the palm of his hand across his trademark snow-white crew-cut stubble. Were he not of such slight build, the warmth in his eyes and smile beneath that white hair and bushy gray eyebrows would have made him a perfect stand-in for Santa Claus.

While Fred spoke of the lake and its more notable residents, Jane sat quietly, if a bit self-consciously, on the stool. It was as if she were non-existent amid the banter of the people enjoying the company picnic. Her isolation struck a chord. I saw myself in her. I was among co-workers, but I felt isolated, strangely disconnected.

I made my way across the wide-decked boat between small groups of chatting people and introduced myself. In contrast to Fred's bubbly tenor voice with its cheery lilt, Jane's was surprisingly deep and gravely, almost gruff, as was the deceptive look on her face. But it took barely a moment to learn that there wasn't a thing gruff about this whisper of a woman. Small talk quickly yielded to words that mattered as she reminisced happily about the travels she and Fred had enjoyed in their forty-plus years of marriage, their grown sons, Fred and Bob, and her sheer love of life. One topic led to the next and before long she had me laughing as she related the antics of a pet raccoon that had brought both entertainment and consternation to their country home near Battle Creek. Like Fred, Jane was just good folks.

At the peak of her health and youth many years earlier, Jane probably stood no taller than 5'1," and when pregnant, couldn't have weighed much more than a hundred pounds. But now, at seventy, she was especially tiny. A heavy smoker for too many years, she had already lost one lung to cancer and had emphysema in the remaining lung. She took air in raspy gulps. Breathing was an obvious chore. But, she said with a certain defiance and pride, "I have already outlived what doctors said and I have no intention of giving up on life until I am good and ready!" She looked over at Fred and her eyes finished her thoughts. She was not ready to be apart from Fred despite the fact that she was still sneaking a puff every now and then and he knew it.

I saw Jane and Fred two or three times over the next couple of years at formal office functions. Fred served on the Kellogg Foundation's board of trustees and dutifully attended every event. They always welcomed me like a long-time friend. Jane would take my hand or touch my arm and invite me to come out to the house to hear more stories about the pet raccoon. Confined to the house much of the time because of her weakening condition, she needed the diversion that a visitor might bring. I promised I would come.

Months and months passed. I was caught up in my own life, young marriage, and personal pursuits. But it was more than that. For as kind as Fred and Jane were to me, I worried that maybe I shouldn't intrude on their lives. They were so gracious and I felt so insignificant. Maybe they were just being polite. Who was I to take up their time? I didn't keep my promise.

Then, one October morning in 1988, a message to all staff flashed across the computer screen in my office.

"Jane Sherriff, wife of trustee Fred Sherriff Jr., is hospitalized," it read. "She fell at home and was taken to the hospital for examination. While there appear to be no broken bones, she suffered a brain seizure at the hospital. A coma has been induced to prevent brain damage. We will keep you apprised of her situation."

A tidal wave of sadness – and guilt – swept over me. I had not kept a promise and now it might be too late.

Then began in earnest, the visits that I should have been making when Jane and I could have shared our stories of the raccoon she had raised, the baby rabbit I rescued from our dog, her beloved swans, my orphan robin, and a host of perhaps now never-to-be-discovered shared interests. Two or three afternoons a week, instead of heading right home after work, I drove to the hospital to see Jane. Each and every time, Fred was at her bedside or talking with the nurses, asking what he might do, what he could do that would bring her out of the coma that lingered after the drugs were withdrawn. He spoke to Jane, held her hand, stroked her hair, and watched for signs that she might be emerging from a world that words and touch seemed unable to penetrate.

In mid-November my supervisor and I made a presentation to the board of trustees on an area of foundation grant-making interest. As the one responsible for having done the research and writing of the report, I studied board members' faces to gauge their reactions as my supervisor presented the findings. Through it all Fred was far away, glancing politely in our direction only now and then. He was in the room no more than his physical presence required. His very being was in the intensive care unit of the hospital. Fred was with Jane. Forty-nine years together had made these long weeks of separation unbearable.

After the meeting ended, board members, officers, and a few staff members took seats in the foundation dining room to visit informally over lunch. I was pleased that I had been assigned to sit directly across from Fred at the very end of a long table close to the windows. The tan brick walls of the community hospital were visible from my vantage point.

Fred ate slowly and deliberately, barely raising his head to make eye contact with other people at the table. On occasion he would nod or smile to acknowledge the conversation that he was barely hearing.

What should I say? What could I say?

Midway through the meal, he stopped eating and I watched him push remaining morsels of food back and forth across his plate. He glanced abjectly out the windows. After a long silence and a deep sigh, he bent forward just slightly, looked into my eyes and said softly, "She might come out of it today. I might go to the hospital from here and find that she's back with us. It could be today."

His green-gray eyes then looked beyond me as if he were speaking to someone other than me. And perhaps he was.

It wasn't that day that Jane came back to Fred, but several days later. A tracheostomy had been placed in her throat to help her breathe. She held onto life by a delicate thread. When I would stop to see her, no matter whether it was during the lunch hour or after work, Fred was there. Sometimes he was dozing in a chair, sometimes reading a newspaper, and sometimes just quietly watching her. She couldn't speak except with her eyes, which spoke volumes. All was as well as it could be when Fred was beside her.

Sometimes the Sherriff's younger son, Bob, came to visit between work responsibilities. Bob had joined the roofing business with his father. His brother had chosen a different career path and lived out of state. A good-natured blend of his folks' best attributes, Bob strode into the room

with a wink and a kiss for his mother. He told her about things of conse-
quence and things that just filled in the spaces. It wasn't what he said
that mattered, it was that he was there and his voice was sweet music.

Extended hospital stays have a way of making the days meld into an
endless blur. To help Jane make her way back and get her bearings, Fred
and I made an over-sized calendar for her room. First we marked the days
until Thanksgiving. Then we began the countdown to Christmas, talking
to Jane each day about the approaching holiday.

Next to the calendar was a poster of two little children dressed as
bride and groom, leaning toward one another and kissing. Beneath the
poster was the date, June 16, 1989. That date marked a milestone that
only a few reach. Fred and Jane's fiftieth wedding anniversary was just
months away.

As Christmas drew closer, Jane was able to take soft foods by mouth
and was beginning to speak awkwardly, just enough for us to understand
her wishes. One evening, a week before Christmas, Fred sat near the
calendar and pointed to the twenty-fourth. "What is this day?" he asked
Jane, pronouncing each word with special emphasis.

She thought long and hard, forcing an idled brain to do her will.
"Chris... mas... eve," she said with great determination.

"And what is this day?" he asked, pointing to the twenty-fifth, visibly
thrilled that things were coming back to her.

Again Jane had the right answer. "Chris... mas... day!"

It was a glorious moment, but not nearly as glorious as the one that
followed. She reached out and gripped my hand to be sure she had my full
attention, then pointed to Fred. Summoning every ounce of strength, she
said, "Fred... Fred... I love *him*!" We cried, we rejoiced, but none quite
as much as Fred. His happiness at that moment knew no bounds.

In mid-January Jane was permitted to go home, despite the certainty
of the hospital staff that had cared for her for so long, that it would not
work. Fred had endeared himself to the nursing staff, but coming to the
hospital every day where someone else provided round-the-clock care
was a different matter than becoming a round-the-clock caretaker oneself.
How could Fred, in his early seventies, care for her at home? It would be
too much for him. Hospital staff members were certain of it.

A tube had been surgically placed in Jane's stomach. She was given medications and a liquid supplement through a stoma or stomach "button." Fred would have to mix the supplements and medications with absolute precision under sterile conditions before feeding her through the stoma. He would also be solely responsible for suctioning her tracheostomy to keep her airway clear. Her care meant adjusting his entire life to her constant needs. The nurses demonstrated these tasks and watched as he learned to do them for Jane. He did them well, yet among themselves the nurses whispered that it would only be a matter of days and Jane would be back in their care. They admired Fred for his unflagging devotion and determination. But there were some things that love just could not do, and caring for her at home, the nurses were certain, was one of them.

But the nursing staff had underestimated the power of Fred Sherriff and his love for his wife. When mid-March rolled around, Jane was still at home. Fred's college engineering degrees had come in handy. He could mix her supplements with confidence that the proportions were precise, had contrived a custom wheelchair, and had assumed his new role without hesitation. Jane could barely talk, but there was color in her cheeks and when she was too tired to follow Fred about the kitchen in her chair, she followed his every move with her eyes. Nurses and aides relieved him for parts of the day and night so he could get some rest, maintain some semblance of his regular daily routine with the roofing company, and resume his daily swim at the Y Center.

Swimming was as much a trademark part of Fred Sherriff as was his closely-cropped hair. He thrived in water, a love that began under the tutelage of the high school swim coach, Leroy Sparks, whom he deeply admired back in the 1920s and 1930s. As a teen, Fred was the captain of the swim team for Battle Creek Central High School and had never lost his love for water.

But swimming was important for many reasons beyond physical fitness. It was a way to relieve stress, challenge himself, and honor coach Sparks. At the age of sixty-five, Fred competed for the first time in a cross-lake marathon named for Sparks. The mile-plus swim across Battle Creek's Goguac Lake was so exhilarating he'd been doing it every year since then, despite the protestations of Jane who always waited anxiously on shore. Each year he covered the distance triumphantly. Fred needed to swim. It was a part of him.

But now his life was more complicated than he might ever have imagined. Some might have complained. But not Fred Sherriff. If anything, he became more resolute in his determination to care for Jane as the days ticked away and their fiftieth anniversary drew closer. As he swam laps in the Y Center's pool he thought of her, of anniversaries past, and of his hopes that they could make it to fifty.

Now, after all the times that Jane had asked me to come to the house to visit in the past, I came. Each time as I knocked at the door, Fred met me with a boyish smile, and each time for as happy as I was to be there, a twinge of guilt came with me for not having come when Jane could have told me herself about her life and her love for their home overlooking a pond, woods, and rolling hills. I sat beside her and watched as Fred mixed her supplements, checked her temperature, and talked to her as if they'd been conversing for hours. What little she could say was difficult to understand, but she tried. She often spoke with her hands, motioning toward Fred, then looking at me. "I love him!" were the words she said most.

The dining room of their home had been converted to Jane's bedroom. A hospital bed faced the big picture window and the back yard that sloped off to the pond and woods. When Jane wasn't in her chair she was propped in the bed so she could gaze out the window to pass the time. Always, there was the *arshh arshh* sound of her labored breathing through the opening in her throat.

It was difficult sometimes for me to be there when Fred suctioned the tracheostomy. I had to turn away or leave the room as the thick mucous was pulled from her bronchial tubes. It was an uncomfortable necessity that showed on her face every time he had to do it. It pained Fred, too, but he did what he had to do quickly and gently, all the while reassuring her that everything would be all right and he would be done soon.

"I worry that I will not do it just right," he confided to me as he finished the process during one of my visits and stood beside me at the window where I had retreated, wondering if I could find the courage to do that for someone I loved.

"I don't want to hurt her. I would never want to hurt her," he said.

When the necessary discomforts were endured, he washed her face, combed her hair, massaged her paper-thin skin with warm baby lotion, and gazed down at her as she rested. It was a special privilege to be a witness to those moments when their love was as sweet and pure in the air as the scent of the baby lotion.

One evening toward the end of winter after Fred had finished Jane's last feeding for the day, suctioned her airway, given her a sponge bath, and tucked her in for the night, he and I sat by the hearth of the open brick fireplace in their wonderfully welcoming kitchen.

"How did you and Jane meet?" I asked,   as we sipped from steamy mugs of coffee. The glow on his face outdid the glow of the fire as he began to reminisce.

Fred Sherriff, February 1994

"My sister Betty, and Jane were roommates at the University of Bridgeport in Milford, Connecticut, back in the thirties," he began. "My sister was getting married and was going to have the ceremony there instead of coming back here, so my family went East for the wedding. I was in my late twenties and wasn't married. Hadn't found the right girl or maybe hadn't really looked. I don't know." He grinned shyly, ran his hand across his stubble-top hair, leaned forward in his chair, set his cup on the hearth, and said, "I remember going upstairs to my sister's room. When I opened the door there was this girl jumping up and down on the bed. She was like a little kid. That was Jane. Jane Souder!" His eyes twinkled. "That was the first time I saw her."

Scuttled out of the girls' room so they could get ready for the ceremony, Fred and the others waited in the parlor where the wedding was to take place. "We were just making conversation to pass the time until the wedding started," he recalled, "when the minister turns to me and says, 'Fred, why haven't you gotten married? Or don't you intend to?'"

The young man was caught off-guard and fumbled for words. "Well I guess… I guess I'm not married because… well… who would marry me?" Fred said innocently.

At that precise moment, a tiny feminine voice spoke up loud and clear from directly behind him. "I'll marry you!"

The tiny voice belonged to tiny Jane and two years later, in 1939, after an extended courtship, much of it by mail, they were married in Battle Creek. Their two sons were small when Fred was called to serve during World War II. Sent to Kiedrich, Germany, the eternally-homesick husband and father was away from home for two years. Jane, then living on the East Coast, tended home and family and watched for his letters.

The letters came, and in them Fred wrote of his work in military engineering, and to his surprise, his role as the honorary mayor of the village of Kiedrich.

An American as mayor of a Germany community during a war?

"Most of the males from the village were either serving in the military or were in prison," he recalled. "So I was named mayor. I arbitrated disputes mostly."

Lucky enough to return home safely when the War ended, Fred Sherriff moved his family to Battle Creek.

"We lived in the city but I wanted to get out in the country," Fred said. "I didn't know it at the time, but when we put our house up for sale, my father bought the house that belonged to the people who wanted our place so they would have the money to pay us." He looked into the fire, perhaps wishing he could thank his father again for his kindness, then added solemnly, "Jane told me she intended that when her time came she would die in this house, right here."

Fred grew quiet for a moment, the impact of his own words settling heavily on his shoulders, then raised himself slowly out of his chair to step to the door of the dining-made-bedroom to listen for Jane's breathing. After a moment he tiptoed to her bedside and smoothed around her shoulders, a quilt made especially for her by the employees of the roofing company. When he returned to the kitchen he eased himself into the chair once more and studied my face, perhaps to see if I had grown tired of hearing about his memories.

"Is everything okay?" I asked.

"She's sleeping," he nodded, sighing deeply.

"You take such good care of her," I said. "She's lucky to have you."

He seemed embarrassed, as if praise was not something he deserved.

"I can see why you'd want to live here," I said nudging the conversation to pick up again, but in a more comfortable place than we had left it a moment earlier. "This is a wonderful place to raise a family."

He glanced at me and a smile crinkled the corners of his eyes. "Oh yes," he said. "It is."

"There isn't anything in the world that means more to Jane than our two boys," he began, his voice a blend of nostalgia and delight. "Every fall we went up north to Trout Lake to bird hunt. Jane almost always went with us, and even went out in the field on the hunts. She loved to watch the dogs work the tall grass in those big circles to flush up the birds." He cut the air with his hand, back and forth, back and forth, imitating the way a hunting dog works the fields. "Jane was happiest when she could be outdoors with her boys, and that included me. I was one of her boys!" He started to chuckle with such obvious delight that for a few moments he couldn't get the words out. "Jane even gained a reputation as being my best bird dog because somehow she could sense as well as any pointer when a pheasant or quail was hidden in the grass ahead. Don't ask me how she did it, but she did it!"

We chuckled at the imagery of Jane on point for a bird as Fred added with gusto, "She was a good bird dog... but she was no retriever!"

Each time he added a piece of wood to the fire he recalled something more from their life together, and as the warmth drifted across the kitchen, Fred relived good times. I learned of Jane the astute bridge player, Jane the flower arranger who could turn garden flowers or ordinary weeds into stunning arrangements. I learned of Jane the community volunteer. He took great pains not to point out any of his own qualities that complemented Jane's so well, including years of being a Scout leader, community volunteer, woodworker, and community historian. His recollections were focused on Jane.

But sometimes in the midst of his journeys through time, Fred fell momentarily silent, reminded perhaps that from this point forward, memories were all there would be.

Winter became spring and spring became summer. On June 16, 1989, without the fanfare that often accompanies fiftieth wedding anniversaries, the Sherriff family celebrated the milestone that Fred and Jane had reached, albeit precariously. It was a bittersweet day, but Fred was intensely happy.

The days of summer gradually slipped away and it was evident that Jane was slipping away too. Her body became unable to rid itself of excess fluids. The edema caused her once wrinkled, sallow skin to fill out and take on a deceptively youthful glow, especially noticeable on her delicate soft cheeks. Jane seemed to be acquiring a cherubic look with impending reason.

Fred would lean over the safety rails of her bed, cradle her face in his hands, and kiss her lips with the tenderness of one touching something very fragile. As he stroked her hair, she looked up at him, wanting to speak what she now struggled to convey with weary eyes.

One evening when I was there, visiting with Fred as he completed his ritual of loving care for the evening, he bent low over Jane's bed to kiss her goodnight. The golden light from a nearby lamp cast a peaceful glow across her face. As his hand rested on her hair he turned, looked up at me and whispered ever so softly, "Isn't she beautiful?"

Summer yielded to autumn and on September 19, 1989, Jane yielded too, dying at home, right where she wanted to be, with Fred at her side. She was seventy-three. He was seventy-seven. She had lived eleven months after her fall, the brain seizure, and the coma. She had lived to mark a fiftieth anniversary. And, she had lived to accomplish one more goal that no one knew she had until after her death.

Jane had written her "boys" a letter after her diagnosis of lung cancer. In the letter Jane spoke of her wishes that her funeral be very simple with a closed casket and that her "boys" not spend hours at the funeral home to greet callers. The service was to be brief.

"Please have the minister say in some way that I don't want any grieving as I have had more happiness from my husband and sons than most ever have, even if they live twice as long."

But Jane had chosen to move on in early autumn with deliberate reason. In her devotion to Fred and the boys, she knew if she were still alive and in need of constant care when hunting season came, they would not make their much anticipated, traditional annual bird hunting trip up north. Her passing at that time made it possible for them to go. How did they know she had chosen autumn as the time to leave? More than a year before her death, Jane had written, "At the end of the service, could the minister read the enclosed verse by William Carruth? It is a favorite of mine..."

A haze on the far horizon,
The infinite, tender sky
The ripe rich tint of the cornfields,
And the wild geese sailing high
and all over upland and lowland
The charm of the goldenrod
some of us call it Autumn
And others call it God

And so on the first official day of autumn, Jane Sherriff was laid to rest in a small cemetery near Yorkville, Michigan, on the shores of Gull Lake. As the pastor read the words of her favorite poem, eyes turned skyward as a flock of Canada geese flew overhead in salute to one whose spirit sailed with them.

Fred's daily routine, that had changed so dramatically when Jane fell ill, changed once more. Now, instead of planning his day entirely around her needs, suddenly he was uneasily free to do as he wished with no schedule to keep and only silence to greet him when he unlocked the door at evening time.

He resumed his work, although on a reduced level, leaving more of the business matters to the care of son Bob, as had become the case when Jane's care had required so much more of his time. He continued going to the Y Center to swim, perhaps as much to burn off restless energy as to keep in shape for the annual August marathon swim across Goguac Lake. Jane had pleaded with him to give up the marathon not long before her fall. But it was too much a part of him to give up and now he felt that he needed it more than ever. Over a lifetime of swimming he'd likely covered hundreds of miles. At seventy, he had been the oldest swimmer to compete in the event. Now, in 1990, as he marked his seventy-eighth birthday he wanted to keep swimming.

Fred swam in 1990 and again in 1991 when this time, son Bob and grandson Ben, swam with him to the cheers of family and friends. Although his fourteen-year old grandson and forty-seven year old son easily out swam him, Fred didn't mind a bit. He was competing only with himself.

When 1992 rolled around Fred had a special goal to aim for. This time he was not only the oldest swimmer, but the only one in his age group, the eighty to eighty-nine division. The distance was the same as the previous fifteen marathons he had completed – 1,650 yards.

When the race ended, all three Sherriff men emerged from the water, tired and chilled. Ben and Bob recovered quickly, but Fred shook uncontrollably for more than an hour as his body protested the demands he had placed on it. Still, he had reached his goal, although Jane would not have been happy about his quest.

"When Jane was upset the best thing to do was just leave her alone for a while... a long while," Fred recalled somewhat sheepishly. "She would have been real upset," he admitted, about his insistence on continuing to do the swim.

In 1993 when August came around, Fred stood near the water, not in it, as the annual Goguac Lake swim began. He itched to be among the swimmers as they warmed up for the event. Being on the sidelines as an observer was one of the hardest things he had ever done. But good judgment outweighed passion in this case.

"I think I could make it across," he told a newspaper reporter that day, "but I don't think it would be so smart." Still, he had to be there to cheer on grandson Ben and that he did with great zeal.

Although his role in the roofing business was less prominent, Fred remained involved in the company, working closely with Bob and continuing to hold the position of president and chief executive officer. He was at the office nearly every day. Life went on. Differently. But it went on.

One late afternoon in early February 1994, I was working around my home when I was seized by the urge to see Fred whom I hadn't visited in a few weeks. I had made no advance plans to visit as I usually did. Something said I just had to see him.

He was delighted when I called. A fire was burning in the fireplace when I arrived, rekindling memories of the fireside chats we'd had way back in 1989.

"I can't retire," he said as he sat in his rocking chair in that cozy kitchen that held so many reminders of Jane. He propped his feet against a sturdy low table, sometimes rocking, sometimes just sitting. "I don't know what I would do if I retired." But talk of the business part of his life was quickly pushed aside as his words and thoughts turned to Jane.

"I have wondered if I took good enough care of her," he said, gazing into the fire. "I hope I did." He talked of how she had said she would never live in that house when he first suggested they buy it and then was determined that it was where she would die. He spoke of travels they had enjoyed and her unflagging devotion to her boys. And he spoke of how upset she got at times — and how he knew when it was best to just stay out of her way until the storm clouds passed.

"Divorce was never an option for us though," he said proudly. "It was something neither of us ever considered. We just always worked it out." He ran his hand across the white stubble on his head and sat quietly, a forlorn and faraway look stealing over him. Neither of us said anything for quite some time. Neither needed to. He looked tired, very tired.

"Fred," I asked, feeling once again a curious, inner prodding, "May I photograph you?"

He was at first reluctant, the shy side of him coming to the fore. But he also seemed pleased to have been asked and permitted me to make a few images as he sat by the fire. I felt honored.

That evening I gave Fred a draft of a story I'd written after Jane's death. It was this story, most of it anyway. It was the story of Fred and Jane and what I was privileged to know of them in those few short years since the pontoon ride on Gull Lake. Fred was delighted and promised to let me know what he thought of it.

I never got a chance to find out what he thought. Two weeks later, just days after his eighty-second birthday, Fred passed away. It wasn't a touch of the flu telling him he needed to rest, as he thought at first. It was the touch of time saying he needed to do his resting in another place, a place where Jane has no cancer and the lake swims are heavenly.

Most love stories have happy endings and this one would too, if it had an end.

But this is a story of love everlasting.

God's Birthday Gift to Mom

For our mother's seventy-ninth birthday in early 1995, my sisters and I planned a surprise party using her favorite color, lavender, as a theme. We decorated a sister's house with lavender streamers, bright purple balloons, and hand-drawn posters rich with the lavender hues of crayon and markers. One sister bought bouquets of lavender carnations that matched a tablecloth, candles, and napkins of the same shade. Another took great care to decorate a birthday cake in lavender rosebuds and another brought a silk floral arrangement of purple pansies in a lovely lavender basket.

It was an absolutely beautiful day for mid-February in mid-Michigan. The roads were clear, making it possible for the family to journey from hither and yon to be together. Dad, who suffered from congestive heart failure and bone cancer, mustered every bit of strength he could to be part of the fun. He and Mom delighted at the boundless energy of their eighteen-month-old great-grandson, Tyler.

When it was time for Mom to open her gifts, she was thrilled to find a set of new lightweight dishes and matching glasses in a lavender iris pattern to replace the heavier dishes that had become painful for her to handle with hands weakened by arthritis. She opened packages containing a purple pullover sweater, an amethyst necklace, and even a cassette recording of the song "Deep Purple."

Throughout the day we laughed, hugged, teased, played, reminisced, and shared the joy of being family. Nephews wrestled on the carpeted floor. Nieces got new haircuts from a sister who doubles as the family beautician. Cameras snapped, food disappeared, memories multiplied, and love deepened.

As evening approached, we all gathered around the large dining room table for dinner. With heads bowed and hands clasped, Dad offered thanks, asking the Lord for a special blessing on Mom for the nearly fifty-five years of marriage they had shared, for the selfless way in which she had devoted herself to her family, and for her goodness as a person.

As we lifted our heads, the evening sun was dipping below the horizon, reflecting its last brilliant rays upward to the heavens lined with tufted clouds. As we all watched in silence, the western skies turned from soft pink to the richest, most beautiful lavender any of us had ever seen, bathing the earth in a peaceful glow.

God had answered Dad's birthday prayer.

Remember Who You Are

"… no matter how hard it gets, I want you to stay in school. You are going to make something of your life. This is who you are. It is your dream. Remember who you are."

The little boy had cut his arm while playing, and the more he cried the more frightened he became. The sight of his own blood and the stark surroundings of the hospital emergency room frightened him. Janis understood his fear. A nurse was attending to a cut on her leg and Janis too had been afraid, at first.

"You'll be more careful about where you play next time, won't you young lady?" the nurse said. "No more stickball in the alley." She told the youngster to wait while the doctor wrote out a prescription.

Janis peeked around the privacy curtain at the little boy who still sobbed. His forehead was sweaty and his grimy shirt clung to bony shoulders.

"Would it be all right if I talked to him? He's kind of scared," she asked the nurse. If the nurse had doubts about how much comfort a twelve-year old girl with a bandaged leg could be to a child with a bleeding arm, she didn't let on. "Certainly," she said.

Janis pushed back the curtain and stepped up to the child. Maybe it was the fact that they both had dark skin or maybe it was that they were both just kids. Or, maybe it was the gentle way she touched him, genuine concern flowing through her fingertips like soothing balm. The sobbing subsided. By the time the nurse began to examine his wound, the little boy was sitting quietly. He said nothing, but the light in his eyes spoke volumes as Janis promised him he would be all right.

Janis has carried the memory of that light with her for more than thirty years because it was at that moment that she knew she wanted to become a nurse.

"I had done something that made a difference to someone!" she beams. "Me, a kid from a Chicago ghetto."

Janis' mother didn't belittle her dream, not even when, after she had just turned thirteen, Janis begged to keep a couple of medical books her mother happened to get through a book-of-the-month club. The books had been sent for trial examination. She studied them over and over.

"My mama had lots of emotional problems," Janis remembers. "Life was a constant struggle for reasons I never fully understood. She was white, my father was black, and she didn't want my father to be a part of our lives when they split up, so after a while he stopped trying. Sometimes he sent me little gifts, but for the most part he didn't come around. It was Grandma Tee Tee, his mother, who was my anchor. I spent as much time as I could with her in Indiana."

Raising her arms into the air and tipping her head back, Janis grins. "She would lift me right up off my feet and say, 'My precious baby, you are somebody and God loves you.' Grandma Tee Tee loved to have me read aloud from her old Bible. When I insisted I was going to be a nurse, she would 'ohh' and 'ahh' and clap her hands together."

But Grandma Tee Tee could not be there to protect the child from the men who came around her troubled mama. The "touching" started when Janis was just five years old and there was no escaping these men who were so much bigger and stronger than she.

"I gave birth to my first child when I was just fourteen and to my second two years later," she says with a voice that is heavy, yet resolute. "Mama wanted me to give my babies away, but I could not bear the thought of anyone raising my children even if it had not been my choice to become a mother."

Still a child herself, Janis kept them both and with Grandma Tee Tee's constant encouragement, also stayed in school.

Before graduating from high school, Janis and her little ones moved to Michigan City, Indiana, where Grandma Tee Tee could help with the children and with the continued dispensing of loving advice.

After graduation, Janis and her children moved into their own place, next door to a woman who had a couple of sons about Janis' age. As the saying goes, no one had two nickels to rub together. Entertainment was a card game in the evenings when the hectic pace of the day had slowed to a manageable crawl.

When it was the little ones' bedtime, John Crittendon, one of the neighbor boys, would accompany Janis and the children home or watch from the front porch until they were safely inside and the lights came on.

"John was a gentleman and was protective of me and my children," Janis says, the corners of her eyes crinkling as she smiles.

Now and then John would ask her to go out on a real date, but Janis always turned him down.

"I don't think of you that way, John," she'd say, not wishing to hurt his feelings. He was a good friend, not someone to fall in love with. What she felt for John was sedate and secure, not bells and whistles and the rush of emotion that the romance novels said love was supposed to be about.

While John waited patiently in the wings, Janis met a charming man who set her heart on fire with promises of the perfect life they'd have together – they and the baby she was soon carrying.

"Grandma Tee Tee tried to talk sense into me," she recalls as only the voice of experience can. "I can hear her yet saying, 'My precious baby, the desires of your heart may not be what God has in mind for you. Sometimes we are blinded by love and don't see a person's shortcomings. The one who loves you will always be there.'"

But young, headstrong, and sure she knew better than her grandmother, Janis didn't listen.

"It wasn't until I walked in on a conversation between my sweet-talking boyfriend and a friend of his that I saw through his glib words. He had no intention of spending a lifetime with me, my little boys, or his own baby."

Some women might have hoped that if they could just love their man enough, just be "good" enough for him, or even just give in to his every whim that they might make such a relationship bearable and, if nothing more, keep a roof over their children's heads. But not Janis.

"My own lifetime of hard times had strengthened me. I had made it this far alone. I could keep right on going even if I was just nineteen with only a high school diploma, two children, and a third on the way!"

The pitter pat of young love was turning into the hardened heartbeat of determination. She might be poor but she was not going to be anyone's fool.

Through it all, there was John Crittendon, right next door, still patiently waiting. "Janis, now will you go out with me?" he asked for the umpteenth time even knowing that she was carrying another man's baby.

"This time I said yes," Janis says with a sudden softness. "I knew he must really care for me."

Janis Crittendon

The birth of Janis' third child, a daughter, brought a double blessing. Unbeknown to her, through Grandma Tee Tee, Janis' estranged father had been kept apprised of everything that was happening in her life. The grandmother had been encouraging him for years to take a more visible role in Janis' life in spite of her mother's resistance. Now, her father reappeared.

"Maybe you don't need a father anymore, but I just want to be your dad," he said, hesitant to push himself into lives where he may not be wanted. His tentative hopes were answered with open arms.

To Janis' enormous delight, her father and John took to one another like long-lost buddies. She found in her dad, a man whom she respectfully says, "loved family until they became friends and loved friends until they became family."

John Crittendon and Janis were married in January 1983, moved into a brand new house in Kingsford Heights, Indiana, and soon began adding to their own brood – five boys in eight short years. As the battalion grew, the barracks shrank. The notion of having enough room for the bare essentials much less the luxury of personal space or a moment of private time vanished as quickly as a batch of warm cookies.

"I was needed by someone for something every waking moment. My own thoughts, not to even mention my dreams of becoming a registered nurse were lost amid being Nurse Mom and contending with heaps of laundry, stacks of dishes, and, 'Mom, I need…, Mom, where is…, Mom, can I…?'"

Janis does not speak with regret, but with the mature acceptance that her lot in life had been drawn and it was her job to fulfill it.

Still, she admits, an uneasiness tugged at her. *You're a good mom, Janis. You're a good wife, a good daughter, and a good granddaughter. You're giving everything you have to everyone else. But who are you to you?* "My life was completely full and curiously empty at the same time."

She shared her frustration with a friend.

"Jan, why don't you go back to school?" the friend nudged.

"Me? School? You must be kidding!" Janis whooped. "I have eight kids, no money, and high school was fourteen years ago. Tell me you are joking!"

The friend wasn't. She nudged again and again, her words a loving elbow in the ribs.

Thoughts of the dream deferred stirred more and more often in Janis' mind.   Sometimes she picked up those old medical texts from years earlier and flipped through the pages, remembering how she would curl up on her mother's couch reading again and again, the descriptions of muscles and organs, blood flow and air flow, symptoms and treatments, fascinated by every word.

What do you want me to do, God? she silently prayed, remembering Grandma Tee Tee's words. *Nursing is the desire of my heart but I have no idea where or how to begin. Show me*!

She applied to a nursing program but was promptly denied admission. *Okay*, she reasoned. *It must be that God doesn't want me to become a nurse. This must be another desire of my heart that isn't part of His plan!*

But the dream persisted.

It was a full year before she had the courage to apply to Purdue University North Central School of Nursing. The Student Support Services office at the University directed her to sources of financial aid. She labored through form after form and by the time the process was completed she had been selected to receive academic support from a dozen separate scholarship programs.

But before she could start nursing school, Janis had to bolster her general academic skills-level. The University placed her in a "bridge program" to brush up on math, science, and English. That process took another two full years.

Still, when she transferred into the School of Nursing in 1995, she failed her first two classes. Sometimes she woke at night in a sweat, thinking, *What am I doing?*

The Student Support Services staff assigned a tutor. Janis repeated both classes, not just passing them, but making the chancellor's list for academic honors.

"Nursing school was the hardest work I had ever loved. It was something I was doing for me," Janis says. "It was me. God was working things out." A classmate who lived nearby offered to give her a ride to campus which was a blessing. Through all her years of changing diapers and chasing toddlers, Janis had never learned to drive.

One of her professors spoke with a strong foreign accent that was difficult to understand, compounding the complexity of the material. A friend suggested she tape the professor's lectures so that she could listen to them on her own time until she understood the material. It worked.

"After doing poorly on an exam, I was discouraged," she admits. "But my professor looked me squarely in the eye and said, 'Janis, of the forty students in my class, you are one of only five who really understands the subject matter. You are not a test-taker, but you will make a good nurse!' My flagging spirits soared!"

Life was absolute chaos. John and the kids would just get adjusted to her class schedule about the time the semester would end and a new schedule took its place.

Then Janis' world, however chaotic, fell apart.

John had not been feeling well for some time. Long hours at his industrial job were difficult enough, but Janis needed his help at home.

He was tired. She was tired. Doctors diagnosed the discomfort in his chest as asthma and gave him medication. But he felt progressively worse.

"John, I don't think you have asthma," she began to nag. "I think you need to have your heart checked."

"Oh, don't bother me with all that stuff you read in class!" he scolded. "There's nothing wrong with my heart."

But there was. After he was rushed to the hospital with crushing chest pains, the doctors ran a battery of tests. His discomfort had come from a series of mini-heart attacks that had left his heart muscle permanently damaged. He could no longer work.

A growing family, Janis in school, and John permanently disabled. If it's true that the Lord never gives us more than we can handle, apparently Janis was not yet at overload because trouble struck again. Two of her classmates died as the result of a horrible car accident on their way to class.

This isn't fair, God! she railed. *They worked so hard. They had so much to offer. Was it all for nothing?*

She unloaded her angers and confusions on her father one evening as they shared a rare quiet moment together. "I don't know if I want to be a nurse anymore," she confided. "What is the point in working this hard if all a person is going to do is die? Maybe it is better if I just take care of John and the kids. I have to quit nursing school, Dad," she said.

His response was swift and certain. "Jan, no matter how hard it gets I want you to stay in school. You are going to make something of your life. This is who you are. Remember who you are."

Janis had no idea those words would be among his last. A massive heart attack. Gone only days later. Age sixty-three. Her dad. Her hero.

She slipped into a deep funk, moving numbly through the days and listlessly through nursing classes. Well-meaning church friends and classmates asked over and over, "Jan, are you okay?"

"Oh sure, I'm just fine. Fine," she mumbled, feigning a smile to make the inquiring faces disappear. But after weeks of lying to them and to herself, she knew she was not okay. *How much am I sacrificing to become a nurse? None of this makes any sense anymore.*

Janis was stumbling around the house one drizzly Saturday afternoon trying to make headway on some housecleaning when her three youngest boys came on the run.

"Mom! Mom! Come watch *The Lion King* with us!" they chirped. "Pl-l-lease!" One grabbed her hand and another ran to get the videotape. They snuggled amid pillows on the living room floor.

The boys chattered as the story unfolded. Without realizing it, Janis found herself drawn in as the king of the beasts is lured into a trap. As the king lies dead, Simba the young cub, tearfully nestles beside his fallen hero. Her own tears began to fall. *Oh Simba, I know just how you feel.*

The boys grew silent, looking up into their mother's face as the tears trickled down her cheeks. "Mama, Mama it's okay," they soothed. "Simba's gonna be okay."

But the tears refused to stop and Janis was keenly aware of just how worn down she had become amid so much uncertainty. In that moment, she made a decision. *I must quit nursing school!*

The boys bounced up and down, bumping against her sides, jolting her back to the present. "Look Mom, Simba's going to be king!" They squealed with delight. Much of the movie had passed by while Janis was swirling in the whirlwind of emotions.

In one magnificent moment, Simba strides supremely to the mountaintop overlooking all the animal kingdom, remembering a time as a young lion when his wise father had instructed him that he must always, "Remember who you are."

"*Remember who you are, Janis. Stay in nursing school. This is who you are.*" Janis could hear, unmistakably, her own father's voice. And then Grandma Tee Tee's whisper, "My precious baby, you are somebody and God loves you!" And close behind Grandma Tee Tee's, the steady voice of that professor saying, "You aren't a test taker, but you'll make a good nurse."

Janis' boys thought the crush of hugs and kisses she lavished on them meant their mom was happy for Simba, the new king of the beasts. They hugged her back, their eyes aglow with a special light.

"I've seen that light more than once since that rainy Saturday afternoon," Janis says. "I have seen it on the face of a heart patient who needed someone to listen to his troubles and who rested much better after we had talked and prayed together. I have seen it in the eyes of an elderly man who asked me at 4 a.m. to call his daughter so she would be with him when he went to join his Lord. I saw it in the face of the president of our hospital when he presented me with the Complete Caregiver Award. But I first saw it many years ago in the eyes of a little boy waiting in a hospital emergency room."

Today, Janis Crittendon is wife, mom, daughter, granddaughter, grandmother, and registered nurse. But that's not the end of the story and earning her degree was in no way the end of the hard work. John's heart condition makes it impossible for him to handle the work he once did, making Janis' income the mainstay of the family. There are teenagers in the home, and even with the conversion of the garage into additional living space everyone could use more room. There is her daughter whose choices as a young adult have not been what Janis might have hoped for, making tough love difficult, but necessary to help her become the kind of woman she has the potential to become. There is never enough time in the day to do all that needs to be done and not nearly enough energy to do it, especially working a nearly twelve-hour shift, six days a week.

"It is the same book. It is just a different chapter," she says with a trace of weariness in her voice. "But I want to see my family prosper."

While the challenges continue to be many, so too, do the blessings. Since Janis' story first appeared in print,* she has been asked to speak many times to offer encouragement to other young women who have endured child sexual abuse and/or have become teenage parents.

In April, 2002, Janis Crittendon, the one-time struggling bi-racial student who some faculty said would never complete her academic program, was honored as a distinguished alumna by the University and its student support services division.

"I walked across that stage in full academic regalia, just the same as the very people who said I would never make it," she says, not with haughtiness but with the hope that those who have been quick to judge her because of her race, her past, or her struggle, may think twice about making such judgments about others.

Janis Crittendon's graduation day
Photo: Purdue University
North Central Publications

"I don't want anyone to underestimate me or their own abilities," she says, "I want to be able, when the Lord asks, 'Who will do?' to say, I will."

*Janis' story was first written on assignment for *Guideposts* Magazine. See, "A Chance to be Me," September 2000.

Revenge of the Selfish Pie

"Every berry you pick you can keep for yourself," she cajoled.
"I will make a pie just for you.
You won't have to share it with anyone."

Every summer when my sisters and I were growing up, my mother made us go wild blueberry picking at the Cedar River marsh. I hated blueberry picking with a passion! It wouldn't have been quite so bad if the runty berries had not grown in mossy marshland on low-to-the-ground, scratchy bushes that seemed to stretch forever and ever into an endless horizon, punctuated only by scraggly evergreens. We would leave home in the morning, taking pails seemingly the size of bathtubs. Our lunch was in brown paper bags. Once we parked the car and headed into that wilderness we didn't emerge until late afternoon. I dreaded it. I loathed it.

In spite of my contempt for the process of getting blueberries, I had no trouble eating them in the form of the jam, sauce, and best of all the pies my mother made. Mom made the absolute best blueberry pie in the whole world with melt-in-your mouth flaky crust. Blueberry pie was my favorite, hands down.

But going through all that drudgery to get the berries was just about more than I could possibly stand.

"Do I have to go-o-o?" I'd whine. "Why can't I stay ho-o-ome? I wanna stay ho-o-ome."

My dour disposition was enough to make even me crazy and I was the one carrying on!

"Stop whining, young lady," Mom would say over and over, trying to be patient with me out in the marsh. "The faster you pick, the sooner we can go home. Look at how well your sisters are doing. They have their pails half full already, and they aren't complaining."

Out came my lower lip and from Mom's lips came a standard line in the Corey household. "Keep your lip stuck out like that and a bird is going to come along and build a nest in it."

Grrrr.

Once, when Mom informed us at breakfast that we would be going to the marsh that morning, I tried sneaking away on the pony and hiding out in the woods until after the rest of the family had left. Surely she would not waste valuable blueberry picking time looking for me!

But to my chagrin, about the time I thought it was safe to emerge and trot confidently home, here came Mother marching toward me on the trail leading out of the woods with one of those you-are-in-trouble-young-lady looks on her face. My parents never laid a hand on any one of us girls when we'd done wrong. They never had to. One look was all it took and she sure had that look.

"You take that pony back to the barn, get your clothes changed, and get in the car now!" she ordered. "You are going blueberry picking, Janice Lee Corey, and don't you think you're not!"

You knew you were in deep trouble when Mom or Dad used your middle name and even deeper trouble when they added the "Corey." I was in de-e-e-p trouble this time.

My skinny legs clung to the pony's sides as he galloped furiously for the barn. Minutes later, I joined my sisters in the car, rode in pouty silence to the marsh, and picked berries for approximately half a lifetime, hating every minute of it. Even Mom's attempts to humor me by asking me to sing for her, claiming she "just loved (my) wonderful singing," didn't improve my sullen mood.

Mom's tactics changed the following summer when it was berry-picking time.

"Every berry you pick you can keep for yourself," she cajoled. "I will make a pie just for you. You won't have to share it with anyone."

"Nobody? It's all mine?"

"Nobody. It's all yours."

"Not my sisters?"

"Not even your sisters."

"Okay!" I said, already thinking selfishly ahead to how good an entire blueberry pie was going to taste. I could almost see it with the vanilla ice cream slowly melting down the sides of a steamy warm slice, then a second, maybe even a third. It was enough to carry me through an entire day of back-breaking berry picking, watching *my* berries mount up in *my* pail as visions of *my* blueberry pie danced in my head. There was a dandy crop of wild berries that season and the picking was easy. Mom had plenty of berries to bake, freeze, cook into jam, and put up in quart jars for the winter.

True to her word, that very evening mother baked a pie just for me from the berries I picked and even etched my name right into the sugar-sprinkled crust.

"Since we have plenty of pie to eat fresh right now, why don't we freeze yours so that when you want it at some special time you can take it out and eat it then?" she suggested.

Her motherly logic made good sense and I watched proudly as she wrapped my pie in aluminum foil, marked my name on the top, and tucked it into our big freezer on the back porch.

"There," she said, as the lid came down with a thud. "It's right on the top when you want it."

Several weeks later, long after blueberry season had ended, my sister Lois and I got into another of our typical sibling squabbles. There were times when I rebelled against her teen-age superiority.

I know what I will do, I schemed with devious delight. *I will get my pie and eat the whole thing right in front of her and not share a single bite. She'll be so jealous. That will show her!*

I made a theatrical production out of going to the freezer and removing my frozen pie. Lois pretended not to watch, though I was sure her mouth had to be watering as I knew mine was. I could almost taste that sweet, juicy pie and oh how I hoped she could too. But she would not be getting any of it! Not so much as a morsel!

When I was certain that Lois was not following me, I scooted upstairs to my bedroom. I opened the foil just a bit to let the pie thaw quickly and slid the dish under my bed.

Ah ha! She would never think to look under my bed for it. Who would ever put a pie under a bed, right? After a few hours – maybe after barn chores later in the evening — I would make sure she saw me eating a big juicy slice without so much as an offer of a taste.

Just to be certain she didn't nose around my room, I made a point of lingering there that afternoon, reading and playing with my Barbie dolls and model horses. Lois would pass my room on the way to hers without speaking, wondering, I was sure, where I had hidden the pie.

I guarded my turf until I could stand being indoors no longer, then went out to ride the pony. Lois was preoccupied with something else. My plan had fallen nicely into place.

Later, each of us did our evening chores then headed for our rooms to read as we almost always did before bed. The pie was now completely mine to enjoy. The rift between us would mend as all our squabbles did eventually.

A couple of weeks passed.

"Girls?" Mom called up from the bottom of the stairs one Saturday morning. "Get your rooms in order and put your dirty laundry in the hamper. I am going to start the washing."

I began gathering things together and knelt to lift the bedspread to reclaim stray socks. My hand bumped up against a foil-covered dish.

Oh no… oh no!

The quite-thawed, very soggy, somewhat-moldy, long-forgotten pie was no longer fit for anyone to eat. Not one slice. Not one gloppy, yucky, greenish bite.

I tried to sneak the mess downstairs to the kitchen and out the back door without being seen, but peals of distinctly-Lois laughter made it eminently clear I had failed.

"How come you're not eating your pie, Jan?" she taunted. "Better eat it allllll by yourself!" Her brown eyes sparkled with last-laugh glee.

God had given me a taste of selfish pie.

* * * * *

All of that happened long ago, but I was reminded of it when my husband and I purchased several acres of woods and wetland adjacent to our pasture. Mom was ecstatic to discover that high-bush blueberries and huckleberries grew in abundance at the edge of, and into, the wetland. The discovery landed her in seventh heaven because since she and Dad had moved away from the Upper Peninsula, she missed her summer jaunts to the Cedar River marsh where she had once held my sisters and me captive for those entire days of blueberry picking.

The bushes along the wetland were likely from nearby domestic berry farms and seeded in the wild by birds. The berries were much easier to pick and twice the size of those I remembered from my childhood days squatting and complaining in the marsh.

My dislike for berry picking had only slightly mellowed in adulthood. Except for the handfuls I would grab from the back of my horse when I passed by on our lane

Mom in her glory

through the woods, I never deliberately went berry picking – not even on my own land on my own terms. And Mom, remembering my great disdain, didn't ask me to join her for what to her was still time spent in a "little piece of paradise." She would pack her own lunch, park her old blue station wagon in the woods, and pick berries alone for hours, happy as a lark. When she would show up at our door later with steamy pies hot from the oven, the bony elbow of guilt would jab me in the ribs as I savored the fruits of *her* labor.

In mid-summer 1999, when the berries were at their peak, Mom was out of town traveling with two of my sisters. "How are my blueberries doing?" she wrote on a postcard home. "I hope we get home in time for me to do some picking before they are all gone."

I winced. By the time she got back the berries would be past their prime and at eighty-something years of age she would likely be too tired from the trip to feel like scrounging around among the bushes, salvaging what she could.

I will surprise her, I thought. If there was one thing Mom would never have expected me to do in her absence it would be to voluntarily go blueberry picking. It would be worth the effort just to see the look on her face when I did!

I threw on long pants, a t-shirt, my tall rubber riding boots, and a cap.

Pails in hand, I headed for the woods, excited about how astonished she would be when she returned from the trip to find that her complaining-ist daughter, would have blueberry pies already in the freezer! She had done it for us when we were kids. I could do it for her now.

Funny, how all those years earlier it had never once occurred to me that when she picked berries all those hours upon hours she hadn't done it just for herself. She did it for her whole family and that meant her, Dad, five girls, and even the elderly shut-ins she was always so mindful of.

I know I owe her one special pie for sure, I had to admit, remembering Lois' peals of laughter when she watched me slink to the trash with the selfish pie that no one got to enjoy.

The berries were big, the picking was easy, and I was having far more fun than I had ever expected. I moved from bush to bush along the edge of the wetland, singing happily to myself. It dawned on me as I sang, that Mom had had ulterior motives when she'd ask me to sing to her as we picked marsh berries all those years earlier. I thought she had done it because she believed I could actually sing. In her infinite wisdom, she knew that singing would brighten my spirits and hers when I stopped whining!

Mothers are so clever, I thought, smiling to myself as I belted out verses of "Somewhere My Love" and "Red Sails in the Sunset," which were two of her favorites. How she would have laughed if she could have seen and heard me!

I sang and picked until I had a couple of small pails full, enough for two or three pies. But an especially abundantly-laden bush just a few steps out into the wetland caught my eye. It stood on what appeared to be a fairly sturdy mossy mound right beside a strong young tree. Between the mound and me was ragged scrub brush, a moss-covered log that could serve as a bridge, and a few young saplings. If I balanced very carefully I could walk on the log out to the bush, grab saplings for extra security along the way, then wrap one arm around the tree as I perched on the mound to capture that marvelous cache.

Carefully and slowly I made my way along the slippery, partially rotted log. The brownish water stood a few inches deep on either side, under-laden by many more inches of moss, muck, and leaves. The log moved up and down ever so slightly as I put one foot gingerly in front of the other, almost holding my breath.

Was my sense of balance not quite what it should be or was I just less willing to land on my backside in the water than I might have been way-back-when? Gone was the brazen I-can-do-anything confidence of my youth.

Could I really do this?

But that bush fairly dripping with big berries called to me.

One precarious step at a time I inched along the log, grateful for each sapling that provided reassurance along the way.

When at last I reached the mound, I let out a great sign of relief. With the lightweight pail looped over my wrist, I embraced the tree for stability with my left arm, and reached out with my right to glean berries from the bush. They were big, at the peak of flavor, and absolutely perfect! The sun was soothing, though I wished I had thought to wear long sleeves to protect my skin not just from its rays but from the scratchiness of the brush and tree bark.

For as much as I had always hated berry-picking, I was having a glori-ous time singing and picturing the look on Mom's face when she learned of my adventure on her behalf. My bucket was filling quickly and by cling-ing to the tree and being careful of the weak spots on the mossy mound, I was managing quite well.

Now and then I leaned my cheek against the warmth of the tree. It was wonderful to be this close to nature and the smells and sensations of the woodland. I kept picking until the little pail was as full as I dared try to carry back out of the wetland.

Relinquishing my death-grip hold on the tree, I again made my way back along the log, one precarious step after another, alternately watching my precious pail of beautiful berries, finding footholds, and grabbing for reassuring support. Just a few more steps and then…

Terra firma at last!

I ducked to make my way through the scrub brush as I let out a whoop that sent red-winged blackbirds, crows, and maybe even a hawk or two winging for other parts of the woods. Triumphantly, with my blueberry booty in hand, I marched along the lane through the woods, across the horse pasture, back into our yard, onto the deck, and into the kitchen.

"Wow," my husband said when he came into the kitchen later and saw my hard-won haul as I rolled pie dough. 'You really did a fantastic job!"

The anticipation of a similar reaction from my mother was almost more than I could stand. But within only a matter of hours, so was the itching. It began first along the underside of my left arm, then fiercely on my left wrist.

Finally, there were golden pies in the freezer, and after a second picking two days later, even a fresh one with a delicate flaky crust waiting on the kitchen counter when Mom returned from her travels.

But there were also red spots from my upper arm to my left hand and smattered across my puffy left cheek and flaming eyelid.

In my eagerness to surprise my mother by bringing home an abundance of blueberries, I had also brought home a passel of poison ivy. The tree I had clung to as I gleefully pulled berries off the bush had been brightly decked out in leaves of three and I had not paid it an ounce of attention as my left arm and cheek cuddled this nasty nuance of nature.

I painted myself with sticky pink lotion and every time my husband looked at me he had to stifle himself.

"I told you so," were not words I would have listened to with lady-like grace.

Mom was nearly speechless when she returned home to find that I had voluntarily gone blueberry picking, not once but twice, with several perfect pies to prove it. Her joy lessened both the pain of the poison ivy and my sense of guilt over the selfish pie of long ago.

But please, don't tell my sister Lois about any of this. There is no statute of limitations on having the last laugh.

CAT – GMC

"How far you go in life depends on your being tender with the young,
compassionate with the aged, sympathetic with the striving,
and tolerant of the weak and the strong.
Because someday in life you will have been all of these."
-George Washington Carver

Every face has a story to tell, but some have a way of letting you know they have not just one or two, but easily a thousand, hidden among their creases and crinkles.

Such a face caught my attention the December morning in 1999 that my husband and I stopped at "Plundersville," a roadside antiques and collectibles shop in Eudora, Arkansas.

An absolutely endless accumulation of things, descript and nondescript, stretched from shelf to shadow, counter to cubbyhole, and restroom to rafter. The store's business card was apropos. It bore an outline of the state, followed by images of an R, a can, and a saw, and beneath that the word "Ever-Thang."

And ever-thang was there in triplicate, including quite literally, Rs, cans, and saws. There were wooden Rs, metal Rs, and plastic Rs. There were oil cans, milk cans, and trash cans. There were cross-cut saws, chain saws, and keyhole saws.

Plundersville wasn't at all orderly, which was, of course, entirely by design. Such places work best if they are in disarray because order takes the fun out of discovering amid the dust and the smell of musty basements and motor oil, the thing-a-ma-jig you've always wanted though you might not have known it was what you wanted when you first came through the door.

To your eternal delight, you find a treasure tucked among some of these and a pile of those, and feel a certain smugness about your eagle eye because surely the shop owner has no idea that he even had what you have found, much less a clue as to its value. What you don't know is that he knows precisely what he has, where you found it, and how much he has to have for it (which is less than what he will tell you at first). It's all a game and everyone plays it with great panache.

But I'm wandering off on a tangent as surely as most folks do when they venture into Plundersville.

Cat Williams

To notice any living thing, most of all a slight, silent black man, amid the array of stuff in Plundersville was remarkable. But there he was, seated on a low chair at the end of the main sales counter about half-way back in the store. He was wearing a heavy blue, yellow, and red plaid shirt, baggy jeans, and a brown and yellow cap that advertised land leveling and surveying in Bastrop, Louisiana. He had a neatly trimmed, more salt than pepper beard, a mustache that had crept right up into his nostrils, charcoal wisps of hair along his cheeks, and woolly eyebrows. His perch at the end of the counter afforded him the opportunity to study over every person who came through the front door and, if a sale was made, to take note of everything they bought. But mostly, if anyone was apt to share a word or two, he was in the right place to hear what was said, though at first it seemed as if conversing interested him not in the least.

"Hello," I said, as my husband and I approached the counter. I was a bit chilled, vigorously rubbing my hands together, even though this was "down South" where folks from "up North" somehow expect it to always be warm.

The old fellow didn't say a word, not a single solitary word, just sat motionless with silence buttoned right up to his neck along with his shirt. His eyes, a bit fogged by cataracts, were so dark they revealed nothing of what he might be thinking, only the mere fact that he had noticed me. Seeing me shiver, he eased into a slow, closed-lip smile that skewed ever so slightly off to one side, and in slow motion, gestured with his left arm across the room to a woodstove.

That's it, I thought, as I watched him gesture. *He can't talk. Maybe he can't hear either, but he can see that I'm cold. It's awfully kind of him to offer me the comfort of the stove.*

"Thanks," I said, maybe a bit more loudly than necessary, as I smiled, maybe a bit too much, to be sure he knew how appreciative I was as I headed for the warmth of the woodstove. I felt awkward, uncertain whether I should attempt to strike up a conversation just in case I might be wrong about his not being able to speak. I didn't want him to think I was rude. He glanced at me a time or two as I warmed myself by the stove but still said nothing.

My husband and I explored the nooks and crannies of the store that seemed to go on forever with its narrow pathways weaving between wagon wheels and kitchen utensils, battered boxes and banged-up kettles, gas station signs and company advertisements, canning jars and medicine bottles, car parts and spare parts, implements and whatchamacallits. There was a little bit of well, ever-thang in Plundersville.

"If y'all need ana-thang y'all jist let me know, won't ya?"

A tall, round-tummied white man with a broad smile that revealed beautiful teeth appeared from somewhere. He was as much a study in contrasts as his store. His waterfowl-bedecked shirt said bird hunter or at least nature lover, but he was gripping a golf club. His cap, in contrast to the black fellow's, read, "Greenville Country Club."

Just to the right of the quiet man, still sitting silently at the end of the counter, was a plastic grass fairway at the end of which was a cup that kicked the ball back to the golfer wannabe after each putt. The tall man putted the ball again and again while his companion went right on sitting silently, just taking it all in – one golfer, two tourists, and a store full of ever-thang.

My husband and I chatted with the bird-shirted golfer for a few minutes while the black man sat with his hands neatly tucked between his knees, almost like an obedient child. All the while we chatted I felt a curious urge to run back to our van for my camera. There was something about him that I wanted to capture on film. But would he mind? Would it be an invasion of his privacy?

Seeing nothing in the entire huge warehouse-like caverns of Plundersville that we couldn't live without, or at least didn't want to cart all the way back to Michigan, we thanked our hosts and headed for the door.

I glanced back as we turned to leave. "Have a good day," I said, not knowing quite what else to say. The black man nodded and offered the smile that skewed off to one side.

We were nearly to our vehicle when I stopped in my tracks.

"Something you saw in there that you want?" my husband asked.

"... a photograph of that man. He had the most wonderful face," I said. "There's just something about him."

"Then you better get going because I know how you are. If you don't, we'll get five miles down the road and you'll be fussing that you didn't do it. Go ask!"

He was right, as usual, when it comes to those sorts of things. I would be kicking myself from here to sundown if I hadn't at least asked if I could snap that photograph.

"Would you two gentlemen mind if I was to take your picture?" I asked cautiously as I went back inside. Maybe one or the other or both of them might be offended. Would the black man feel I was treating him like an object of racial curiosity rather than someone whose face was so compelling? Would the white man think this tourist from the north was making a mockery of his southern lifestyle, (though Lord knows we have plenty of northern versions of Plundersville with far less creative monikers).

Their reaction was not what I expected.

"Way-ll why shore you can take our picture. Whattaya say Cat, can this lady take our picture?" the portly fellow chirped, stepping up beside his friend and laying one arm across his shoulder. "Smile Cat. You're gonna get your picture took!"

I snapped a couple of photos of the two of them at the end of the counter and then standing side by side behind it. With the hodgepodge on the shelves behind and around them, the bird shirt, the plaid shirt and their reflection off the countertop, the men nearly blended like camouflaged hunters into their surroundings. They were as much a part of Plundersville as every treasure in the place.

After snapping a couple more images, I photographed Cat alone. As I moved in for a close-up, a transformation came over him. He stood straighter, smoothed his whiskers like a preening cat, and said quite distinctly, "I am Mister Henry Williams, (with special emphasis on the "Mister") and I live at …."

Cat spoke his name and address much as a child reciting by rote to a teacher, or a soldier barking rank and serial number to a commanding officer. He began to chatter happily in broken sentences, responding to most of my questions about himself with a low "uh huh."

My husband and I lingered. Instead of closing a door to communication, as sometimes can happen when the suggestion of taking a photograph is made, it had very definitely opened one.

"My wife Marilyn and I've been running this place for years," Melvin Ward said as he returned to tapping the golf ball into the little trap. "Cat, here, has been pretty much a part of our lives most of that time. Ole Cat has had a pretty interesting life, haven't you Cat?" he said affectionately.

"Uh huh."

"There ain't nobody around here that doesn't know Cat. He lives with a woman, but mostly just stays here at the store, helping us with wood for the fire and runnin' to get a few groceries or things we need for the store. I've knowed Cat since we both worked on the gin (cotton gin) a lot of years ago. He never was allowed to learn to read and write, so when I send him to the store I have to send a note with him as to what I want."

We visited a bit longer and as we left, I promised to see to it that they got copies of my photographs.

"Be sure you send those pictures now lady," Melvin said. "Cuz Cat here will drive me crazy asking if I have heard from that photo lady from up North until you do!"

A couple of weeks later I put several photos in the mail addressed to "Mr. Henry Cat Williams" in care of Plundersville. One image, set in a gray folder-frame, was a portrait of Cat with his slightly-skewed smile.

I waited a few days and then called Plundersville, hoping the photos had arrived so I could find out how Cat had reacted.

"Shew-ee lady!" Melvin sang when I identified myself. "Cat got that photo and now he is showing it to ever-body that comes through this door! And just like I said, he asked me ever-day if there was any mail for him from the photo lady."

"Cat!" he called out as I waited on the line, "It's the photo lady from up North. The one who took that picture of you. You wanna say hello to her?"

A soft voice greeted me. "Hello photo lady. This is Mister Henry Williams and I live at ...."

"Did you like your photo, Cat?" I asked.

"Uh huh."

We talked awkwardly. Some of his responses to my questions or comments came in partial sentences as before, and always in soft submissive tones.

Melvin promised to send me some information about Cat and his life. I began to eagerly anticipate the arrival of my mail in Michigan as Cat had in Arkansas. A few weeks later a fat envelope arrived. I grabbed it from the box as my husband and I were leaving to run some errands, and read its contents aloud as he drove, occasionally glancing over at him to gauge his reaction. Now and then a tear graced the corner of his eye.

The first bit of writing came from Melvin.

* * * * *

I been waiting on other folks to write something about Cat but I never got it done.

All his life he's spent ten years there, ten years here, five years there, five years here. Just who ever would take care or put up with him. Most everybody it was not for long. Funny how good people (Cat) don't stay long in one place. That's also funny how since good, wouldn't-do-nothing-wrong, naïve, good-natured people get treated really lousy in life. Cat loves everybody.

He's got a birthday June 20th and he'll be 73. We'll have cake, presents that goes with a birthday party. He really enjoys all the attention and wants to know what you're getting him for his birthday. Everybody will be asked that day by Cat, "What did you bring me for my birthday?" His name and age is already outside on the lighted sign at the store. Spelling would be better but wife ain't here to check this.

Thanks,
Melvin Ward and Henry "Cat" Williams

＊＊＊＊＊

Accompanying the letter were four regular-sized sheets of paper, written in pencil on one side, ink on the other, and carefully cut out of a notebook. The penciled text was written by an 84-year old woman whose family had lived next door to Cat when he was a child in West Carroll Parish, Arkansas, in 1927. Her father, the local self-taught veterinarian, had delivered Cat, as he had many other young-uns in the neighborhood, assuming there were more similarities than differences to the birthing process. Even a veterinarian was better than nothing when nothing was the only alternative.

The elderly woman had written:

I Knew a Boy

I once knew a small boy,
Always a smile on his face;
You never knew if he felt pain,
He wanted to brighten his small space
Cat has left many footprints
As he walked on the sands of time;
Each life he touched has a story
Here's just a wee bit of mine....

Sometime in the early forties, I first knew Cat, his stepfather Big Boy, and his mother Ella, when Dr. Green moved them into his potato shed so he would have someone to help with the livestock. Ella would help Dr. Green's wife (my Aunt Dollie) with the housework and she did the job very well. Cat brought in stove wood and wood for the fireplace and helped gather the many eggs that were laid each day.

One day, Aunt Dollie told Big Boy how much she appreciated Ella and the good job she was doing. Well, that ended a good thing for my aunt. Ella never returned to help in the house. No explanation, but later Aunt Dollie found out what happened. Big Boy did not know his wife was helping out and he did not want his wife working. He said he could take care of his wife and Cat.

Few people I know have a memory such as Cat and his mother. They both knew the birthdays of everyone with whom they came in contact and took every opportunity to send birthday greetings to those people. I was always amazed when I would see Cat's mama and she would say, "Tell Nancy Rose or Lottie Mae or the twins, happy birthday." What a talent to have such a memory.

I see Cat now and I am projected back in time to a more simple way of life that some may not want to remember. In that time frame, Cat, or Junior as I knew him, was a small boy with a water bucket in his hand headed for my pump to draw water for their daily needs. He made the trip many times to the hand pump that was near my back door. Frail in frame, but always with a smile, he took his time pumping that bucket full for he did not want to miss anything – a word from me or my husband, a comic movement from my small children, or maybe just a flock of biddies following an old hen.

Their house (Cat's family) stood not far from ours and our hens would go there to lay their eggs sometimes. As soon as Cat heard the cackle of the hen he went under the house and retrieved the egg. I think he must have been well supplied with breakfast food over the three years he lived there.

Cat's childhood could not have been very pleasant. His stepdad was harsh with him and there were times I think fear of him must have been pretty strong. I do know that his stepdad ate first and if there was anything left, he and his mom ate. If not, they went hungry.

What happened to them after they moved is not clear, but often I would see them walking the roads, never together but in a line, Big Boy first, then Ella, and Cat behind her.

He got the name, Cat, while working for the Browns. I'm sure the stories they could tell would fill a book but that is a whole 'nother tale.

* * * * *

Then, on the reverse of those same pages, Melvin Ward shared recollections of his friend, Mr. Henry Cat Williams.

Remember this as you read, Cat did not like to go home. He had a bad stepdaddy. Really bad.

I first met Cat in 1957, working at a cotton gin. Cat was working for the Brown boys. They hauled cotton seed from the gin to the cotton seed plant to be processed into meal and hulls. They never fed Cat too often, so every day I come to work at the gin I'd bring more supper than I would eat while I was at the gin.

I would get off school bus at four o'clock, and eleven o'clock had to go home. Cat worked all day, was still at gin loading cotton seed trucks when I left. Lots of mornings when we would come by on school bus going to school, Cat would still be there loading them trucks.

One evening I got to work about six o'clock. I couldn't find Cat to see if he was ready to eat supper with me. He was nowhere to be found. I went to Mr. Clyde and Mr. Ray, they run the gin and told them I couldn't find Cat. The seed truck was almost loaded but no Cat could be found.

Mr. Clyde and Mr. Ray stopped the gin. We all started hunting Cat. We finally all stop (probably twenty men) at and around the seed truck. I can and always whistled really loud. Cat always would listen for the whistle when we were at the gin. So, I whistled. We all were listening for Cat. No Cat. I whistled again. Someone hears a far off moan or grunt. Sounded way off and it was up in the seed house.

I was the youngest. Up in the seed truck I went. Mr. Ray and Mr. Clyde told me not to go up in the seed house. It was about forty feet high and the seed could cave in on you.

We all stop again when several of us got up in the seed truck to listen again. I whistled again. Sure enough, Cat was buried up in the seed house!

We started digging – the seed kept falling.   We kept digging. Finally Cat's leg! We pulled him out, we poured water on him. Cat was OK now. Me and him went to eat. We saved Cat's life!

Lots of tales from lots of folks. All knew Cat. All loved Cat. He really never and still to this day knows no wrong. Can't read or write – don't know colors. About his schooling, I was told by Mr. Tom, the school bus driver. Mr. Tom took him to school one day, his bad stepdaddy went and got Cat from school, say by now he was smart enough. Cat worked in fields all his life until he got cotton seed loading job.

A tale but true, Brown Boys took Cat over to the levee where they had cows. Some of the fence was down. They pull an ole car to where the fence was down and Cat would spend the nite in that ole car, keeping the cows off the highway.

Cat was what we all call down here as "easy." Easy to get him to do anything but he didn't want to go home, bad stepdaddy. Everybody enjoys Cat at my store. He tells them he's the "Big Black Boss" and he runs this store, him and "Big Boss Lady" (my wife).

Cat learned down at the gin a saying that was as good as you ever heard only if you know a little about Cat.

The trucks they had were GMC. Somebody ask Cat, 'Cat, how you spell GMC?' Cat would say, 'C-A-T... G-M-C'! He loved that rhyme or whatever he thought that was.

C-A-T... G-M-C!

Cat sits back by the wood heater reading the paper or any kind of paper or book I give him. Now we all know Cat can't read and he is color blind. But I got busy one day (in the store). Cat, like always, was in his chair reading the newspaper. People was everywhere. I went back to where Cat was. He had the paper up in front of his face. I put my hand on the paper, I said, Cat, you come help me. He looked up at me and said, "Just as quick as I finish reading paper I'll be there!"

Nobody ever comes in the store that don't speak to Cat and he will sure speak back. Everybody loves Cat.

I just bought a refrigerator and stove. He didn't want me to

*leave up front, said he would put price tags on appliances. Well, he
did. He got them backwards and I changed them. He's gone to get
WD-40 for me. I have to send an empty can with him cuz he can't
read. He'll come back with hard candy and popcorn. Everybody
gives him everything.*

*Well, he just got back with the WD-40. He signed the invoice
CAT. He is something really special to all of us.*

* * * * *

After receiving the wonderful personal stories about Cat, I made
another call to Eudora, Arkansas. It was just a day or two past Cat's
73rd birthday.

"Cat, it's the photo lady from up North!" Melvin chirped when he
heard my voice. "She called to wish you a happy birthday! Come 'n talk
to her, Cat!"

Once again a soft voice greeted me. This time he said, "It's my birthday, photo lady. I am Mister Henry Williams and it's my birthday. What
are you gonna give me?"

"It's your birthday, Cat?" I asked, feigning surprise.

"Yessum."

"You'd like me to send you something?"

"Yessum."

What would you like me to send you, Cat?"

"Uh huh."

"Are you saying it doesn't matter, I should just send something?"

"Yessum."

His voice sounded for all the world like a voice from America's past.
A voice that had been conditioned to show deference to white people.
It was something to which I was not accustomed and did not want to
become accustomed. Cat owed me nothing. If anything, it was I who
owed him something.

"Well Cat, I will send you something really soon. Is that okay?"

"Yessum."

With that, Melvin came back on the line and said people had seen
the birthday sign out front of the store and had flooded Cat with gifts and
best wishes.

"He was as happy as a kid all day long," he laughed.

"What can we send him for his birthday?" I asked.

My husband, standing nearby as we spoke, pointed to his head, grinned, and mouthed the letters G-M-C.

"Does he have a cap that says GMC?" I asked Melvin.

"Nope, I don't reckon he does."

"He will now!" I said, winking at my husband.

And so he does. A cap that reads, CAT - GMC.

He shows it to ever-body who visits Plundersville.

"I am Mister Henry Cat Williams," he begins, "C-A-T... G-M-C."

No Less Than Forever in Mind

"There is something about this barn, its age, its character. I get the feeling it is bigger than life. It is inspirational to me. There is life here."
-Glen Noonan

What in the world would lead a man to quit a high-paying, high-profile position in an East Coast company, uproot his family and move them to Michigan? Why would he take the family's savings and buy a neglected old barn?

Love. And maybe even an old "spirit" with a new agenda.

"I still don't know what it was that made me quit. There were people who would kill for the job I had," Glen Noonan says, his eyes dancing. "But I went to my boss one day and quit. Just like that."

For Glen and his wife, Wendy, moving to Michigan was a homecoming. Glen had been born and raised in the Leelanau Peninsula's Maple City, and Wendy in nearby Traverse City. Glen wanted their daughter Lisa, and son Joshua, to grow up in the area they knew so well.

The Noonans were packing for the move when Glen's father called from Michigan with exciting news. The old Gilbert farm, next door to the Noonan family farm, had just been put up for sale. The farm was a place Glen had known and loved since childhood, especially its barn. Glen had not known the farm was going to be offered for sale when he had quit his job. This was a complete surprise!

"I had one week to make up my mind about the farm," Glen laughs as he runs his fingers through thick, blonde-brown hair. He admits that it took a lot of persuading to convince Wendy she was "lucky" to become the co-owner of an exhausted barn and tired house sixteen miles west of Traverse City on M-72.

Built in 1889 by William Gilbert, the main section of the hand-pegged, gambrel-roof barn was forty-by-fifty feet in size with seventeen-foot wide, lean-to sheds on both sides. The barn and sheds were built of the hemlock, pine, and oak that grew in abundance on the Peninsula when Michigan's logging industry was in its heyday in the late 1800s and early 1900s. The barn's pine verticals were set on two-by-fours of oak as were its upper rafters. Hemlock "one-by" beams were set on oak and were so hard a nail could barely be driven into them. For many years a wooden-stave silo graced the southeast corner of the barn.

William Gilbert built the barn to house his Holstein dairy cattle and the hay to feed them. The barn served its intended purpose throughout the forty-one years Gilbert farmed and for some years after son Herald Gilbert, and wife Laura, took over the operation in 1930. Herald eventually stopped tending dairy cattle and converted to vegetable farming, mainly potatoes. The two and a-half-foot thick, native fieldstone foundation of the main barn was ideal for year-round cool storage. A good-sized pumpkin patch between the barn and the main road attracted the attention of passers-by and helped to generate business.

The Noonan and Gilbert farms were separated by only a fence row. Glen fell in love with the barn as a child, climbing and playing on the property line fence. "I always loved that barn. There was just something about it," he says fondly.

But Glen's career took him away from the Leelanau Peninsula for sixteen years and change was under way. The creation of the Sleeping Bear Dunes National Lakeshore meant that an area once overlooked by tourists was now drawing people in droves. It meant that the openness of the peninsula was giving way to homes, and that cattle, potatoes, and even vast orchards of succulent cherries, were succumbing to golf courses and condos. The Gilbert place was sold, then sold again with each successive owner putting less back into it than he was taking from it.

Farms have a way of revealing their sadness rather quickly when they aren't being cared for. Roots creep into foundations, splitting stone and concrete apart. A loose strip of metal roofing or a few torn shingles, allow rain to seep onto rafters and mow floors. Wet wood warps and buckles. Like sway-backed horses, rooflines bow until eventually, barns collapse on themselves, nudged by a heavy snowfall, strong wind, or fatigue. Often by default, neglected barns become above-ground landfills and sites for rodent rendezvous as piles of old this and unneeded that, are discarded in every nook and cranny. Fields, once neat with rows of crops or neatly shorn by grazing livestock, become overgrown and weed-infested. Developers stare hungrily at these icons of the past and in their place, see upscale subdivisions, golf courses, mini-malls, and casinos.

But not Glen Noonan. As sunlight streamed through holes in the roof and warped wallboards, illuminating mounds of clutter, dusty hay, cow manure, potato buckets, scrap metal, baling twine, boats and even a disassembled house, Glen Noonan saw a vision of what the grand old centenarian might become.

"It had been a grand, classic farm, a real showpiece. The farm, especially the barn, was Laura and Herald Gilbert's family because they had no children. They put their love into the barn," Glen says.

The Gilbert barn, put into service on February 24, 1889, officially became the Glen Noonan barn on April 15, 1989, little more than one hundred years to the day later. Glen considered himself its "custodian."

The barn's roof was in such bad shape, the layers of shingles were "like an overheated compost pile" he says. He stripped off the entire roof and replaced it with new shingles set on twelve-inch supports and put a metal roof over that. The metal roof has a life expectancy of at least fifty years and carries a twenty-five-year guarantee. Between the shingled roof and the metal roof is a double layer of insulation. The insulation was put there rather than below the rafters so the beauty of the barn's beams and rafters could be seen from inside.

"There is something about this barn, its age, its character. I get the feeling it is bigger than life. It is inspirational to me. There is life here," Glen says reverently, tipping his head way back to gaze up at the rafters. He lowers his voice and adds, "There are times when I have been working here that I feel someone else is here. Someone is watching me."

Taking a deep breath, his expression remains earnest as he calls out, "Mr. Gilbert?" He glances here and there as if looking for someone, then adds, "He's here and I think he likes what he sees."

For ever so slight a moment, one has the feeling that Mr. Gilbert is there indeed, leaning against a support post, a pair of work gloves poking from a pocket, an appreciative smile lighting up his face.

Glen continues, "It is the little things about this barn that make me know that everything that has happened — quitting my job just as this place was up for sale — it's all happened for a reason."

Glen and Wendy Noonan transformed the Gilbert barn into "The Red Barn Sampler," an eight-thousand square-foot gift and craft store, creating an inviting place of charm, whimsy, and yesteryear. Visitors who may never have seen the inside of a barn, touch original woodwork and imagine what it might have been like to gaze out from its upper floor in the days when land stretched for miles unmarred by human hand.

Tourists climb the wide stairs to what was once the haymow to look at antiques and gardening motifs, wander by displays of gourmet soup mixes, old fashioned preserves, and pause to sniff candles and potpourri. They fall in love with hand-stitched quilts and run a finger lovingly over the top of a skillfully-crafted box made from the boards of a fine old barn that wasn't fortunate enogh to survive.

They explore the tiny room on the main floor painted and decorated to look like a schoolhouse, and as they make their way from cool basement to aromatic hayloft, the visitors to the barn admire its graceful angles and sturdy frame. Perhaps they share a remembrance or two of a barn they once knew. They sense something here: the spirit of a Michigan barn that was built with no less than forever in mind.

Earth Angels Take Flight

"For a long time after Joan and I sold our Florida home and boat, I told people we'd done it because we were tired of taking care of so much stuff. Beneath each feeble excuse ran the powerful undertow of the voice. 'Peter, there is more to life than this.'"

-Peter VandenBosch

Peter VandenBosch had the kind of life most of us can only dream about – excellent health, financial security, a devoted spouse, and happy family. He was also fully retired at the age of sixty with nothing to do but precisely what he wanted to do. And what he wanted to do – or at least what he thought he wanted to do – was to fish, play golf, and fly his twin-engine Piper Seneca II.

The line of folks eager to take his place gets longer until you add that he also works forty to fifty hours a week without pay.

Yes, that's right, forty to fifty hours a week and nothing to take to the bank for it. Unless, of course you count the heartfelt gratitude of people whose lives he and others are helping to save.

I thought, the day I called to ask if he would agree to be interviewed for a story for a healthcare newsletter, that I would learn about his work in the health field. I learned more, much more. This, in his own words, is Peter's story.

*****

I really had it made, you know. Retired at sixty, excellent health, happy family, nice home here in Michigan and a vacation home in Florida, two fishing boats, and of course my airplane. I really did live the good life and I loved it all. But then came that day in November of 1989 that changed everything.

It was two weeks before I could tell my wife, Joan, what happened that day. It was two years before I could even talk openly about it to others. I'm not sure why I kept it absolutely to myself. Afraid maybe? Didn't think anyone would believe me? Worried that others would doubt me and that would lead me to doubt myself? After all, who in his right mind with all I had going for me after years of hard work, gives it up just like that because they hear a voice? Would you?

There were four of us on my boat that day — me and three of my favorite fishing buddies. We were all retired guys, enjoying the good life in Florida. We headed southwest out of Naples on a calm sea. It was an exquisitely perfect day to fish for grouper, just about the best saltwater fish you could hope to catch. It was all just so perfect!

We were moving out at about twenty-five knots or so in the open boat. The noise of the engine drowned out conversation so we all settled into our own thoughts. There is something soothing, renewing about being out on the water, and I couldn't have been happier.

By late morning we put down anchor about thirty-five miles out. There were no other boats in sight and the sea was as calm as I had ever seen it — that glasslike surface people talk about. Each of the guys had taken up a position around the boat so we wouldn't interfere with one another's lines, but we were talking back and forth as we readied our lines to cast out. It was incredibly wonderful.

After a while the conversation faded as we watched our lines. The boat was rocking ever so gently and the water was just barely tapping the sides of the boat. That gentle motion has a way of lulling a person into a silent place within himself. It's one of the joys of fishing. You can sit for hours staring at a line stretching out into an expanse of blue and just think your own thoughts. Sometimes you imagine and long for a big fish to fight you at the end of that line and you play out the battle in your mind. Sometimes you think about the people in your life. Sometimes you just enjoy thinking about nothing in particular. That's how it was that day, each of us lost in our own thoughts.

Then came the voice.

"Peter," it said, "there is more to life than this." The voice was clear, firm, soft, but awesome. "There is more to life than this."

I have to tell you, I grabbed my pole and looked at each of my buddies to see who had spoken. Every one of them was in his same position staring almost motionless at the lines that ran from reels to water. Not a one of them had said a word.

"There is more, Peter!" This time the voice was more insistent.

My knees began to tremble. Me, a grown man with not a care in the world. What in the world was happening? Was I losing my mind? We hadn't been out long enough for the sun and the sea and the wide expanse of beautiful nothingness to be playing tricks with my mind like a mirage on a desert.

"There is more."

I heard it again. I had heard a voice and there wasn't a shred of doubt about it.

For the next several minutes while my friends watched the sea, totally oblivious to what was going on inside me, I replayed the voice in my mind, letting it reverberate like an echo in a canyon.

"There is more… there is more… there is more…."

Later, we returned to Naples with a good catch and went our own ways with plans to go out again soon. I said nothing to my friends about what had happened, nor did I say anything to my wife when I got home. As the days passed, Joan noticed how distracted I had become. What in the world was happening to me?

A full two weeks passed. Still, I was preoccupied with thinking about the voice and still, Joan said nothing. But it was obvious that she was worried about me.

I knew I had to tell her. I trusted her opinion and maybe there was something in what I would say that she could help me make sense of. So, I suggested we take a drive over to Ft. Myers where there are lovely orange groves. She knew this wasn't an ordinary drive on an ordinary day. We packed a picnic lunch and headed out, finding a peaceful spot under the beautiful fruit trees.

This wasn't going to be easy.

"Honey," I said, "there is something I have to tell you."

Joan listened to the whole story from start to finish without taking her eyes off me for even a moment.

When I finished, she sat almost motionless, then reached for my hand and without so much as a hint of hesitation said, "Peter, I think we ought to sell out here and go back to Michigan."

Wow. Sell our home, our boat, our months in the sun by the sea? She was kidding right?

No. Joan was as certain of what she was saying as I was certain of what I had heard that started this whole thing in the first place.

But from that very moment we never doubted, and we never looked back.

We put our Florida property on the market and by February of 1990, the most frozen month of the year in Michigan, we were headed back to Holland where the Lake Michigan shoreline was now a mass of ice jams and bitter wind. Most of our Florida belongings had been disposed of, and what was left went with us in our twin-engine Piper.

Now, don't get the idea that we got home and lived happily ever after. It didn't happen that way. Not by a long shot.

First we were met with a barrage of questions from friends and fellow church members. Why had we sold our lovely home in Florida? Was something wrong in our marriage? Was our health all right? Did we have financial problems? Were the kids okay?

For a long time I told people we'd done it because we were tired of taking care of so much stuff. I complained that I was bored with traveling and lounging on cruise ships, and that the food at exclusive clubs had all started to taste the same. Beneath each feeble excuse ran the powerful undertow of the voice, "Peter, there is more to life than this."

I told people, too, that selling the property in Florida freed us to give more time to our family. And that was true. Joan and I adore our six children and fifteen grandchildren and every moment we spend with them.

I even told people that retirement wasn't so great when you don't have anything useful to do with your time. Friends and wanna-be-business-partners jumped on that like a grouper on a lure. They had all kinds of ideas for how I should use my time.

My career had been in broadcasting. A former business associate suggested that I invest in a radio station again and serve on its board. But no – been there, done that. I had already owned a station and had been its CEO. I loved it at the time but my heart wasn't in doing it again.

"There is more to life," the voice had said.

Another colleague was determined that I buy into a large retail furniture operation. Holland is known for its fine furniture. Investment opportunities abounded. But that held no appeal.

Whatever I did with my time had to be very special. That I knew. But I wasn't sure what I was supposed to do. "There is more...."

Apart from my family, my life had always revolved around three things: my radio station WJBL in Holland, music, and flying. I had formed the Kings Choraliers male chorus in 1950 and directed the group for twenty-three years and at more than four hundred concerts. Music was so much in my blood that in 1963 I founded the one hundred-forty-voice Metropolitan Choir and directed it for thirteen years before standing-room only crowds.

Music sets a person free, and my love for music was matched only by my love for flying. Oh how I loved the freedom of flight!

Let me tell you about me and flying. My dad used to give me that look only a dad can give when I was a teenager on our farm in Minnesota. He'd shake his head and say, "Peter, how do you expect to get your chores done when you're staring at the sky?" He knew that the very instant I heard the far-off rumble of the early '30s, Ford tri-motor, antiquated predecessor of today's jet-liners, I would be straining my eyes to the skies to get a glimpse of it. It didn't matter what we were doing – tending cows, feeding chickens, or hauling hay – everything in the world came to a screeching halt when a plane passed overhead.

I remember telling my father quite defiantly that someday I would fly one of those things. He never doubted it. He knew that when I set my mind to something I did it. I was just like him that way – a take-charge, get-it-done Dutch attitude. So, of course, Dad wasn't the least bit surprised when I became a radio operator on a B-24 Liberator bomber with the 15th Air Force in World War II.

After the War, I used my GI Bill allotment to get my pilot's license. And after that it was difficult to keep my feet on the ground. I was always around planes – bought a Cessna 182 in 1954. The whir of the propellers getting started, that high-pitched whine of the engines revving up, and that positively giddy feeling when the wheels leave the ground, gives me a rush. If heaven is anything like the thrill of flying, I know where I want to spend eternity!

Peter VandenBosch
Photo: Holland Sentinel

Speaking of heaven... another important part of my life is the church, so after I sold the radio station and retired in 1983, I put more time into traveling with the King's Choraliers. Music has always been a way of expressing my faith without talking about it directly. That's the way it always was in our family. Believing was something you did quietly.

So, to get back to where I started— about why retirement and fishing off the coast of Florida turned into looking for work back in Holland, Michigan, in the middle of winter. Talking about that wasn't something I could do very easily, especially when it was based on a voice out of nowhere. But people kept prodding to find out, because none of my excuses had them totally convinced. It got so I was tired of trying to come up with things to tell people because their response was usually, "Are you out of your mind?" I was beginning to think so myself!

Through all of this Joan was patient, never pressuring me to decide what to do or second-guessing our decision to return to Michigan. She just waited. I listened to the offers of friends and scanned the papers for something that I could latch onto that seemed like a good fit for a trying-not-to-be-retired executive. But mostly I just prayed and waited.

"God," I said, "if you want me to be doing something with my life right now besides being with my family, you'll have to tell me. You'll have to make it real plain, because even though I'm listening I am not sure what I am supposed to be hearing. You had to be the one who sent that voice. But what is the 'more to life than this' that you want me to find?"

February turned into March and March into April. Joan was still being patient but I was getting restless. Spring brings that burst of energy, but I didn't know what to do with it. I had to get out and do something. But what? If, in fact, God had spoken to me months earlier, how long did He want me to wait to know for sure what His plans were?

Then came May and the phone call that in thirty seconds would end the waiting. The call was from my long-time friend, Les Slagh. The two of us had at one time owned an airplane together.

"Hey Peter!" he said in his booming voice. "I have an idea...." As Les rolled out a plan, I knew that God was speaking to me again as He had in the boat, and just as He had with Joan the day we picnicked in the orange grove. It was all beginning to make sense.

That single phone call was the start of Wings of Mercy, a not-for-profit organization that provides free air transportation to people who need to get to a major medical center for critical treatment but can't afford the flight. We started out in Holland and grew from there. Wings of Mercy made its first flight in mid-1991, and by late 1998 we had made more than one thousand flights. By 2001 we had four chapters – one for the west Michigan area, another for the eastern side of the state, a third serving Minnesota, and one we call 'Illiana' that reaches into both Illinois and Indiana. We may open a fifth chapter in Missouri.

There are now between one hundred fifty and two hundred pilots all over the state. At any given time they will transport a person in their region along with family or medical staff. Since 1991 we have flown more than two thousand missions and more than 1.2 million miles. Our best estimate is that if there was not a service such as this, more than eighty percent of these people would not be able to get the specialized treatment that could heal or extend their life.

We have transported patients to most major medical centers and university hospitals east of the Rockies. Wings of Mercy requires that there be two pilots on each flight. Our pilots are only reimbursed for fuel. They give their time, training, and the use of their aircraft. We operate on fundraisers, a wing, and a prayer!

Wings of Mercy is staffed by a fulltime volunteer director (that's me) and a part-time assistant. We have an eight-member board of directors to oversee everything we do.

My very first mission was to take two children and their mother from Holland to Rochester, Minnesota, for treatment of a condition that causes both premature aging and cancer. These kids were barely in their teens but they looked like they were well into their eighties. I flew them again and again over the years, and every time, the gratitude that they showed in their hugs and tears was like hearing that voice from all those years ago and knowing now exactly what it meant. "There is more."

Wings of Mercy pilots have become like family to people who are referred from doctors, churches, and social service agencies. It does not compete with air ambulance services that have airplanes equipped for the types of patients that we cannot handle.

My life has a joy and purpose that exceeds any success I ever had in my years as a business executive, and surpasses the pleasure found in anything I ever owned. All of that was just the groundwork for making this possible. This is my life and I am in love with it.

On my desk are hundreds of letters that Wings of Mercy pilots have received from patients and their families. One of my favorites begins, "Dear Earth Angels...."

* * * * *

Glorious artwork often portrays angels as delicate creatures with graceful white wings. It's a comforting image but a limited one to be sure. As a Wings of Mercy pilot helps his or her precious cargo get settled in for the flight to a medical center, then climbs behind the controls, it is wonderfully clear that there is more than one way to describe an angel and more than one way to wear a pair of wings.

Store-Bought Donuts and Florescent Roses

"Mah wife was a good wohman. If I'd wake up of a night with a belly hurtin'
she'd get up and fix me somethin'. You miss 'em when they're gone. Now it's
jist them plastic biscuits from a can. You ever eat them thangs?
Yah cain't eat em!"
–Charlie Warris

There's no mistaking the fact that Charlie Warris misses his wife of fifty-six years. It's the first thing he tells you if you give him half a chance.

The moment I saw Charlie, who has lived all of his considerably long life in Kentucky, he reminded me of my dad's cousin Harvey Warner. It was something about the ruddy complexion, closely-cropped white hair, little round eyes, and the way he perched his black felt hat squarely on the top of his head. I figured Charlie at about seventy-five, though I've never been much good at guessing a person's age.

Charlie Warris

I met him at a wake in eastern Kentucky, in January 2000. A wake, for us Northerners, means stopping by the local funeral home, staying a socially-correct amount of time, and going on one's way. But for a true rural Kentuckian, maybe for other rural Southerners as well, a wake is a community event that goes on for the better part of two or three days and nights, right in the home of the dearly departed if at all possible. Sometimes it's not possible, of course. The house may be too small, too rickety, or too far up a hollow (holler) or across a creek for folks to get to except one at a time and then maybe only on foot, never mind the hearse (which might just be a four-wheel-drive truck if the hill is rugged enough).

Thank goodness for embalming. It gets a tad stuffy in a holler in a house wall to wall with mourners, store-bought donuts, and enormous baskets of florescent roses in every unimaginable shade the dollar store has to offer. The arrangements line the walls and cling to display racks four feet high.

A Kentucky wake is an excuse to take time off from coal-mining, neighbor-watching, and tobacco-tending. It's a time to take note of what the deceased will be wearing to his or her final resting place and to get a real good look at the duds the neighbors have donned as well.

They gather in little groups, the men to one side, women to the other, to drink coffee, jaw and chaw. A new plug of tobacco tucked 'tween cheek and gum just before a fellow comes through the door will last a good long while, maybe not as long as the visit, but long enough. The casket serves as a sort of line of demarcation between the men and the women, some of whom are hunkered in the kitchen keeping the coffee hot and the donuts replenished.

It's no wonder this ritual is called a wake because no one except the deceased is going to get any sleep, especially once the elders of the church take to preaching. And after an hour or two of that, one can almost look at the deceased with a certain amount of envy.

Wakes actually got their name from the fact that family and friends used to take turns staying "awake" all night to guard the casket. Some say the practice had to do with warding away bad spirits, others claim it has to do with keeping people from stealing belongings off the corpse. Considering what I have heard about what goes on in some of the hills and hollers of Kentucky, where it seems people are as suspicious of one another as two hounds eyeing the same bone, I'm inclined to think "awake" is a good idea.

My husband and I made the trip to this holler in Kentucky because Bessie, the wife of his distant cousin, Frank, had passed away. It was my first introduction to a home wake and to Charlie Warris. When I spotted Mr. Warris, he was perched on a chair tucked in a corner of the dining room right beside a dusty oversized buffet crammed with china that hadn't been used in twenty years. Charlie was just enough in the mainstream not to miss a single coming or going. People had to pass directly by him on their way to the living room to view the body or to the kitchen to get another cup of coffee. He could listen to the men, but keep an eye on the women, an ideal vantage point for a man of his deportment.

Charlie's black hat was a statement, not a fashion statement so much as an expression of the importance he associated with this noteworthy event. A wake was a black hat occasion. Nothing was going to escape his attention or that of several of the other elders of the Old Martha Regular Baptist Church. By the time we arrived on the third day of the wake, the men had already spent hour upon hour at Frank's house, some lingering past midnight to swill large amounts of coffee and equally large amounts of gossip, both darkened by personal preference. Some clustered on funeral home folding chairs in a semi-circle near the casket. Others came and went – mostly behind the barn to relieve themselves. Men – it makes no difference – Confederate or Yankee – can't use a bathroom six feet away if they can trudge half an acre behind the nearest barn, garage, or tree, even in the rain. And it rained every day of Bessie's wake. It rained so much that by the time it came time to bury her at the top of the big hill just up the holler from the house, even the four-wheel drives were having trouble climbing the steep greasy incline.

But I'm getting ahead of myself.

Bessie's casket was set on a gurney in front of drawn drapes in the living room that, quite conveniently it turns out, looked for all the world like funeral home drapes. Rose-colored funeral home lamps stood at the head and foot of the bronze-colored casket, casting a warm, comforting glow across her tired face. A portrait of Frank and Bessie was propped in the casket, a reminder to all that once there had been youth and vitality in their aging frames. Bessie had finally succumbed to the diabetes that

The elders

had claimed part of one leg a few years earlier. She had gone steadily downhill after that, still convinced that the leg was there, frequently attempting to scratch the missing foot that still itched. Worse, she sometimes tried to stand, not the least aware until she pitched forward, that there weren't two legs to support her round little frame. That was when the security straps became necessary and the frustrated outbursts increased.

In her glory days Bessie had been a woman to be reckoned with. She could wield a knife the size of a bayonet to butcher a hog as easily as she could prop a shotgun on her shoulder, and with a warning primed on her tongue, send trespassers high-tailing it. She spoke her mind in no uncertain terms.

But a portion of Bessie's mind had taken leave with the portion of her leg, once the diabetes took control. She'd sit in her wheelchair at the dining room table and stare out the double windows to the rock-jutted hill behind the house, point and say, "Thare's two men a'comin' down that hill now. 'Ah wonder what thar a'comin' fer." The only part she had right was the hill. There were no men.

Finally, Bessie just couldn't be taken care of at home any longer, and for her own good and that of the sister who had given up her own life in another state to come and tend to her, had to be put in a nursing home. Even there, her feisty mountain spirit and a conveniently trapped-in-the-past mind kept her going a couple more years. She never stopped talking about the work to be done as if any day she could get right back up and do it as she always had. Frank drove down the holler and into town every day to check on her and make sure she was being well taken care of. He trusted no one and said so in no uncertain terms.

As the elders sat or stood in groups of two or three here and there about the kitchen and living room, church folks and neighbors, even a few strangers, came and went, stopping by the casket to whisper about how lovely she looked and how hard she'd worked "all them yars." Frank, a lanky man in his late seventies, straddling a chair between dining room and living room, would acknowledge their sympathies, glance toward the casket, and say in a quavering voice what a "good little wohman" Bessie'd been to him. Then he'd shift his cud of tobacco, spit in a can beside his chair, and go right on visiting about beef cattle and coal mines and the hard life he figured he'd had. With almost precise regularity he'd step up to the casket, touch the collar of his wife's soft pink dress, and sigh, "Mah little partner."

Meanwhile, Charlie Warris sat in his secure corner opposite Frank, taking it all in.

Not only a Northerner out of her element, but a woman in a decidedly man's world, I hesitated before venturing into the fray. Finally, I could hesitate no longer, but knelt by Charlie's chair to ask if I could snap a photo of him. For a moment he simply looked at me with a mixture of uncertainty and curiosity. He'd never seen me before, perhaps had never seen a camera with such a great long lens, and wasn't sure just how to respond, although I sensed instantly that he liked the attention.

"Come on Charlie, the lady wants to take yer pih-cher!" one of the other church elders chided. "This is yer chance to be famous."

Charlie Warris visibly puffed up and consented to have his photograph made, but the relaxed winsome look disappeared from his face and a studio smile and artificially-high angle to his chin appeared in its place. I snapped a couple of images, taking an extra long time to compose my photos, waiting for the moment when he might let down his guard.

"I was borned in nineteen and a-nine, December the fifth," he said, peeking at me as I fussed with the focus on my camera. "I was marr-eed fifty-six yar and worked thirty-seven of them yar in the coal mines. My wife died not so long ago. She was a good wohman... suffered bad. Sick seven yar. Nev'r got dressed, nev'r combed her har. My girls come and done all that fer me, helping me take care of 'er. I kept her right thar in 'r home. Done it mahself. She was a good wohman."

I didn't have to ask questions. Charlie Warris talked, and talked freely, basking in the chance to be the center of my attention and that of a few of the church elders clustered near the dining room table heaped with store-bought donuts. No doubt they knew every word of his story by heart, but maybe his retelling it for a woman half his age permitted him to tell it again with a bit more panache. They listened and smiled, throwing in a word now and then to spur him on.

All the church elders were men. The Old Martha Regular Baptist Church didn't accept women in a leadership role. A woman's job, according to the elders' interpretation of Scripture, was to fix the soup beans and cornbread for Sunday church dinner, sit dutifully through two-hour long services, put on the dinner afterwards, and clean up the kitchen before they went home to start cooking all over again. The men were to do the preachin,' the decision makin', the hymn singin', and other things, a few of which weren't entirely consistent with the preachin'. That was the way it was and always would be if the men could keep it so. It was a pretty good racket from a man's point of view, and many of the women had never known anything different.

"Mah wife was a good wohman," Charlie went on, his dark little eyes peering down at me. "If I'd wake up of a night with a belly hurtin' she'd get up and fix me somethin'. Now it's jist four walls. You miss 'em when they're gone. She use' ta make me biscuits and gravy. Oh, the biscuits and gravy." He ran his tongue over his lips and let out a great sigh. "Now it's jist them plastic biscuits from a can. You ever eat them thangs? Yah cain't eat em!"

He paused a moment, studied my face, and continued, "Mah daughters live on either side of me and they look out for me. A home's not a home without chil'ern."

The question was coming. The one about, "You got children?" which would be followed by, "Why not?"

It was time to distract Mr. Warris again. I held the camera to my eye, fiddled with the settings a bit, and asked if I could snap a few more images.

Charlie Warris grinned and with a sudden shyness said, "Well all right then." He sat a little straighter, fidgeted with the top button on his shirt, and lifted his chin, striving for just the perfect look, squinting a bit to see if the rest of the church elders were still watching. They were. He puffed up a little more.

"How many of them pih-chers you gonna take?" he asked, as I snapped from first one angle, then another.

"Just a few," I said. "I like to get just the right look."

Others among the elite group of church elders teased Charlie Warris, a hint of envy in their voices that they had not been singled out for such attention from a woman much younger than their own wives and distinctly more cosmopolitan if only because I was from somewhere they likely had never been. The more they teased, the more Charlie beamed until his cheeks had an almost Santa-like glow.

When the picture-taking was over, to his relief I suspect, we chatted a bit more.

"How old you reckon ah am?" he asked. This was a question he had put to others no doubt with great satisfaction.

"Oh, I would guess maybe around seventy-something," I said, fudging slightly.

"Honey, you're lookin' at a man who is ninety yar old." He puffed up like a grouse at a mating ritual and began at the beginning... again.

"Ah were married fifty-six yar and worked thirty-seven yar in the coal mines. Borned December the fifth, nineteen and o-nine. Sure was." He was proud of those years of marriage and work, work and marriage. In all likelihood he was as married to the mine as he had been to his wife and he needed both to survive.

We might have talked a bit longer but it was time for the elders to begin their evening prayer services. Four or five of them moved from beside the store-bought donuts to the florescent roses, Bibles tucked authoritatively under their arms. Several of the women had gone home so that there were more men than women remaining at this house up a holler. It was just past five-thirty.

One by one the elders preached, sometimes walking back and forth before the casket, sometimes rooted in their folding chairs, now and then letting out, in a kind of a mournful wail, an "Oh-oh-oh Lo-o-o-rd" that could make the hair stand up on the back of a person's neck. Or at least on this person's neck. At some point in the midst of it all, the preaching elder would drop to his knees by his chair, the others would follow, and something vaguely resembling a good old gospel hymn would be sung. The lyrics were familiar, but the melody was decidedly original, and each elder sang it his own way, second verse entirely different than the first. An impassioned prayer lasting another several minutes came after the singing, and after that another elder took over amid a chorus of "A-a-men" after "A-a-men, brother."

With each prayer I bowed my head and prayed passionately too, thanking the Lord, that I was lucky enough not to have been here the first two nights. No disrespect intended.

After the first three sermons of the first three elders for the first three half-hours, I slunk into the kitchen to wash dishes, enjoying the experience more than I ever thought possible, glancing now and then at the image of a Bible-wielding, preaching elder reflected in the darkened window over the sink. Beyond that window the big Kentucky hill met the sky that was changing from day to night, enfolding the trees in murky blackness. Wakes, I realized, from my solitary corner, were exclusively an all-male event and excuse-ively a time to stay out very late. I washed the dishes as slowly as I could as another half an hour turtled by. There were still more elders waiting to preach but I had long since run out of dishes.

Charlie Warris was still perched in his same prime location when my husband and I slipped away from Frank's house in the holler into the night. Charlie smiled as we tiptoed to the door, respectful of the deep significance that this ritual had to these people whose faith and means of expressing it were every bit as important to them as ours is to us.

The lights from the living room were muted behind the drawn drapes but cast a glow into the yard as, with relief, we headed for the shortcut across the mountain, back to the motel in Prestonsburg. The funeral in the morning would be a two or three-hour affair and after that would come the climb up the hill to lay Bessie to rest in the family cemetery set against the skyline. From the porch Frank would be able to see the little cemetery where his wife and other kin were buried. Stories abounded about some of those kin, even about the skeleton of a baby found in the bottom of a creek when a man had come to excavate the creekbed with a backhoe many years earlier.

The bones had been gathered together and set in a shoebox on the porch where they became something of a silent ghost, about which everyone sought to concoct a story, until someone took them away. Presumably they too were now in that cemetery on the hill, an unnamed little person whose own truth would never be known except by one or perhaps two people.

Frank, as he had promised when Bessie died, would ring the big old school bell in the yard for fifteen minutes so everyone in the holler would know she had been laid to rest. After that there would be more store-bought donuts and someone from the funeral home would gather up the florescent roses.

The last I knew Charlie Warris was ninety-five yar old, not getting around too well, but still faithful to the Old Martha Regular Baptist Church and its group of elders. One day his daughters will keep the coffee pot hot for the folks who will gather at his little house to pay their respects, preach, and eat store-bought donuts. There will be florescent roses to honor the old Kentucky coal-miner and maybe someone will think to tuck his black felt cap between his tired fingers for the last important wake he will attend before joining his wife of fifty-six yar.

But there'll be nary a plastic biscuit in sight. Charlie Warris will be grateful for that.

The Angel Played a Song

For he will command his angels concerning you to guard you in all your ways.
-Psalms 91:11

Julie and Erick Mowery were awakened in the night by their daughter's screams.

"Mommy! Daddy!" Eliza wailed. She scampered across the hall into their bedroom and leaped onto their bed.

"Honey, it's okay, we're here," Erick soothed, expecting her to calm down after they reassured her that she had probably just had a bad dream. Perhaps the rustle of the wind in the trees outside the windows of their Rockford, Michigan home had frightened her. Eight-year-old Eliza had a vivid imagination. Once her parents had become accustomed to her frequent accounts of the boogie men that surely must be lurking in every sound or shadow, they knew not to be overly-alarmed.

"Daddy, something's wrong!" she cried as she wiggled her way between her parents. "You have to go in my room and see!"

At first Erick only half-listened. She would tell him again, as she so often did, that she had seen something or heard a noise under her bed. He would look under the bed and in the closet, tell her that he had sent the boogie man on his way, reassure her that everything was fine, tuck her in her bed, and that would be the end of it.

But that didn't happen this time.

"My music box is playing!" she said in a tight, high-pitched voice. "My music box is playing all by itself! I'm scared."

This was different from all the other times she had come to them. Hardly the kind of thing a child would make up.

"I'll go see," he said. "You stay close to Mommy."

Erick eased out of bed, ran his hands across the top of his head and over his face to make himself more alert.

A music box playing by itself in the middle of the night? Must have been part of an especially vivid dream.

As he stood up he could hear it. One of his daughter's little wind-up music boxes was playing, just exactly as she said! He hadn't heard the tune for quite a while but it came back to him as he stood in the dusky darkness of the bedroom. "Windmills of Your Mind," was the tinkling tune he heard.

"How in the world...," he half mumbled, turning in the semi-darkness to ask his little girl, "Honey, did you play with the music box before you went to bed?"

She vigorously shook her head. "Nuh-uh, Daddy, I haven't played with my music boxes for a long long time."

"What do you mean by a long time, sweetheart? How long? Can you remember?"

"Not for months and months. Really!"

Eliza pressed herself as tightly as she could to her mother while Julie stroked her little girl's hair, reminded of what a privilege it was to be a mother, even if it sometimes meant being awakened in the night.

"Okay," Erick said. "Maybe it got bumped or something and that's why it is playing. How about if I put it in another room for the night? That way it won't bother you, okay? Want to come with me and I'll tuck you back into bed now?"

"Mmm, hmm," she said softly, crawling out from the warmth of her parents' blankets and the security of her mother's arms.

Erick stepped across the hall, his little girl clinging tightly to his hand. He stayed beside her bed until she had wriggled back down under the covers. He tucked them in around her chin and leaned to plant a kiss on her forehead.

"There sweetie," he said in a voice of quiet confidence. "Everything will be fine. You just go to sleep with sweet, sweet dreams."

As he left Eliza's bedroom, he plucked the music box from her dresser and peeked in on his son, Nick, who was sleeping undisturbed in another bedroom. Then Erick tiptoed into the bathroom adjoining the master bedroom and set the delicate little music box carefully on the counter, taking great care not to jostle it for fear it might erupt into sound again. He stood in the doorway to the bathroom for a moment or two, waiting to make certain everything was all right.

"That ought to do it," he whispered to Julie when all remained quiet, then climbed back into bed, putting his cold feet against his wife's toasty-warm ones. She giggled and nestled to him. Everything was still. All was well.

The couple drifted back to sleep only to be awakened just minutes later. The music box was playing!

"What in the world is going on?" Erick muttered, rolling over and wadding the pillow under his head. "I can't believe this."

Julie sat upright in bed, a surge of adrenaline coursing through her. She was fully awake.

"Honey," she whispered, shaking Erick's shoulder. "I think God is trying to wake us up for a reason. This is no accident!"

Erick sat up. The couple was motionless, listening as the tiny music box played the refrain from "Windmills of Your Mind," over and over. It was as if it had only just been wound up.

"What do you think this means?" Erick said softly.

"I think it means we should check to be sure everything's okay in the house," Julie said. "God is trying to tell us something."

"All right," Erick said. "I'll check around the house. You peek in on the kids again."

He leaned into the bathroom and lifted the music box from the counter.

This time I will take it downstairs. If it insists on playing again we won't have to hear it for the rest of the night.

He moved slowly from room to room checking windows and doors on the upper floor where everyone slept. Julie went to each child in turn and made sure they were covered and comfortable. Things were fine. The children were sleeping undisturbed.

Still clutching the music box, Erick headed downstairs to the main portion of the house, checking windows and door locks, the controls on the stove, even the refrigerator door to be sure it was closed tightly.

He peeked into the garage. No problems. No burglars. No boogie men.

I'll put the music box in the bathroom around the corner, he thought, *and go back to bed. I have got to get some rest.*

He flipped on the light as he stepped into the downstairs bathroom. As he reached to set the music box on the counter beside the sink, with horror he saw blackness beginning to creep up the bathroom wall. The family had all gone off to bed and had left a candle burning hours earlier. Fire was about to break out inside a wall of their house!

The Mowery family had forgotten about the candle. But God had not forgotten and had sent an angel to alert them. The angel played a song.

When Harry Met Hosta

"I'm beginning to have a little more faith in people and in attempts to save nature. I'd like for my grandchildren and my great grandchildren to be able to see things as I have because we cared enough to work to save nature."

-Harry Tadman

In that wacky movie of the late 1980s, *When Harry Met Sally*, the main characters, played by Billy Crystal and Meg Ryan, don't like one another very much at the start of their relationship-of-necessity. But both of them need to get from Chicago to New York, one has a car, and traveling together makes economic sense. They squabble, they bicker. They snip and they snipe. And somehow along the way they fall in love.

Well, that's a little like how it was when Harry

Harry Tadman

Tadman met hosta. Not nearly as romantic, certainly. We're talking about a man and a leafy green plant, after all, not a man and a fair flower like Meg Ryan.

"First time I saw 'em I didn't like 'em," Harry says, with an air of finality, as if the way the relationship began is how it remained. Except that it didn't. Harry loves hosta.

No, wait. That might be a bit of an understatement.

Harry Tadman is passionate about, obsessed with, consumed by, and, quite literally, overrun by hosta. According to his gardening buddy, Ted Kurnat, who would certainly never reveal closely guarded secrets without good reason, Harry is a bona fide "hostaholic." (Takes one to know one.)

Hosta bear no resemblance to Meg Ryan, though both are perennial beauties. The difference is that Meg Ryan seems to bloom all the time while hosta, at least in our northern climes of the Midwest, bloom only once a year.

Hosta can be as small as a teacup or as big as a teacart; they can have tiny little white leaves or great, round blue-green leaves. They can have leaves that curl up or leaves that lie flat, leaves that have ridges or leaves that are smooth. They can be lovely when grown as a single specimen or striking by the dozens. There are more varieties of them than there are movies starring Meg Ryan, and her name is on the marquis for quite a few. A Meg Ryan movie might even be quite enchanting with names like some of Harry's varieties of hosta. He has Pilgrims and Wagon Wheels, Jade Beauties and Blue Diamonds, Crested Surfs and Temple Bells. In his garden it is only natural for a Little Sun Spot to spring up near a big Solar Flare. His Robert Frost grows near Frances Williams and a Patriot is content beside a Loyalist.

Harry Tadman has four hundred eleven varieties of hosta in all, six of which he developed himself through meticulous propagation (something which also eventually occurred to Harry and Sally). Just a few of each specimen of hosta would easily fill a pretty good-sized chunk of garden space, but Harry Tadman will be the first to tell you that when he gets "bitten" by any kind of collecting bug (he's been bitten numerous times) he doesn't know the meaning of the word "one."

"I work in tens," he says with an impish grin that turns down at the corners of his mouth in a sort of a something-more-is-coming quiver. He gestures off toward his garage. Four greenhouses extend one behind the other at the back of the garage like a passel of possums behind their mother. There, thousands of "babies" are lovingly nurtured and readied for "adoption" to other yards and gardens from Battle Creek to who knows where. And what isn't in the greenhouses is gloriously displayed in his yard. There are hosta along the sidewalk, hosta clustered under trees and curving along wood-chip walkways. There are hosta in raised, landscaped beds, each variety carefully labeled. It is easy to see why my mother and Harry have gotten along so well as volunteer master senior gardeners for the local arboretum and why she wanted so much for me to meet him.

Harry's hosta share an acre or so of garden with flower beds popping with perennials, feeders a flutter with the dozen or so varieties of birds that thrive in his backyard, and flowers dancing with hundreds of butterflies and bees. There are three deep, concrete-lined pools to serve as homes for fish and frogs, and deep basins to meet the hygiene needs of raccoons that wash their hands before dinner. Until the bandit-eyed varmints got too demanding and tore a hole in the roof of his house to let him know they wanted free access to the food supply he meted out at his discretion, Harry fed them generous meals of bread and cookies. At one time, his yard was even home to a pair of tame skunks named Petunia and Lilac.

"I fed 'em and talked to 'em," he laughs. "Every animal has a distinct personality. Lilac had to be talked to quite a bit or she'd lift her tail and Lord knows what might have happened, since I never had the pair descented. Petunia, on the other hand, would sleep in my arms."

He keeps one hand on his cane to steady himself as he leans forward in his chair on the back stoop of his suburban home, motioning slowly back and forth at the ground with his free hand.

"If anyone had ever seen me they'd have had me locked up. I'd go around here at night with a flashlight, digging around the gardens to teach Petunia and Lilac how to find grubs. Those two little skunks would look at me like I was crazy."

Frogs and flowers, Petunias and Lilacs, all this in a little piece of paradise most of us would miss as we zoom noisily past on the busy avenue that passes by the Tadman home and is a gateway to Battle Creek's west end. Our eyes are riveted on traffic, our heads are crammed with clutter, most of which isn't worth the attention or anxiety we give it. Life slips by without adequate thought to where we've been or where we're going.

Harry Tadman knows where he's been as he leans back in his chair and looks long and longingly about him. He was born in Battle Creek in

1922 and spent his first few years on a farm just west of the city near W.K. Kellogg Airport on what is now Skyline Drive. Maybe the proximity to the airport explains why, when he was a toddler, there was a canvas-winged, open-cockpit biplane stored in the barn on the farm.

"I'd go out to that barn," he says, his eyes brightening and the corners of his mouth beginning to quiver. "I couldn't-a been more than three or four. I'd climb up in the cockpit of the plane all gray and white with splotches of dried pigeon poop, and pretend I was a pilot."

Harry's grandfather was an engineer on the Grand Trunk railroad that passed the east end of the farm. "My grandfather would blow the whistle as the train rumbled by. Mother would lift me up onto her shoulders and I'd wave to my grandfather. I thought I was pretty big time, I hope to tell you. Pretty big time." His eyes suddenly have the unmistakable sparkle of a child.

Memories of life on the little farm are good for Harry Tadman. Memories of the raccoons, rabbits, turtles, snakes, cats, possums, and pigeons that were his friends. Well, friends most of the time.

Harry and Spike

"We had a rabbit that if you didn't pet it when, or as much as it wanted to be petted, it would back right up and wet in your shoe," he says arching his eyebrows.

But of all his pets, his best friend and protector was Spike, a mutt who never let the boy out of his sight.

"I wandered away from the yard one day when my mother was busy," Harry recalls. "My mother followed the sound of Spike's barking and when she found me I was in the pasture. Spike was standing guard between me and the bull who would have trampled me if it were not for that dog."

Harry was about four or five when his parents moved to the Post Avenue area of Battle Creek from the farm in the country. His father abandoned them soon after, and he did not see his father much after that until he was grown.

"It's all gone now… the house… the barn… that farm. All gone."

He rests quietly for a moment, fingering the edge of a tiny photograph he has fished from a box on a bookshelf. A small boy and a dog are in the center of the old photo, a tall proud barn behind them. "All gone…" he sighs.

But true to his nature, Harry doesn't let nostalgia get the better of him. He places the photograph on a table beside his chair, leaving it and childhood on the farm to return to the here and now.

"This land," he says, nodding toward the yard, "originally belonged to my grandparents." He shifts his cane from his left hand to his right and points in a southwesterly direction. "The Interurban was a train that ran through here from Chicago to Detroit. My uncle was going to put up a little store not too far from here to serve the people who got on and off the Interurban. He had his plans, but he died without fulfilling them.

"My grandma planted the whole piece – all three acres – to peach trees. I used to work in her orchard when I was young. It was my job to pick the fruit. I lived with my grandmother after my step-grandfather was hit and killed in 1939 when he was walking home from his job at the train yards. I was seventeen years old."

We move into the house where he can sit more comfortably, the travails of age and illness taking their toll on his thinning frame. His wistful gaze through the window to the yard beyond, says he is seeing it from another time and place.

Harry is quiet for a moment or two, perhaps just feeling the weight of time on shoulders that can't begin to do what they once did, but would give just about anything to be able to again. It wouldn't matter how hard the work was. He's not the least bit afraid of hard work.

"Grandma gave me this land and three thousand dollars when I was eighteen. I drew up the plans for the house and dug the basement with a team of horses and a scoop shovel that the horses pulled." He leans forward on his cane and flashes that crinkle-eyed grin. "Then I bought a 1929

DeSoto with a hatchback. I took out the hatchback and built a box in its place and for two years I hauled dirt in that box. Oh, did I haul dirt."

A blue jay squawks and swoops from the branches of a towering pine down to a rock near a bed of hosta. Wrens flit from a homemade bird feeder to a bird house not far away from the open window through which his voice drifts to them on the breeze, holding their attention like the melodious sound of a storyteller. They know his voice and associate it with goodness.

The peach trees are long since gone. One would never know they had ever been there. Dozens of other trees have taken their place and some, the evergreens mostly, are now tall and stately.

"Every tree on this land I have planted," Harry says in a voice both satisfied and wistful. The bond between this man and this land is palpable. This is a moment not to be interrupted with words but to just let be so that he can drink in the shadows dancing on the leaves, the smell of the bark, slightly damp from an earlier rain, and the chatter of the birds among the branches. "I know every tree, every blade of grass here...."

Harry shifts in his chair and sighs a long sigh before he speaks again. "Lots of times I feel my grandmother is here. I feel her presence and the presence of others in the house." He studies my face for a bit before he continues, looking to gauge whether I am receptive to the notion that spirits dwell among us. "There are times I have caught a glimpse of a shadow in the hall. My wife Jan, has seen it too. Neither of us is afraid or bothered. It's all right with us." He smiles and his expression grows pensive once more, as if by concentrating hard enough or long enough the spirit might appear. It would be all right. All right indeed.

Then the conversation shifts gears as he again shifts positions in his chair to ease an aching back.

"I worked as a sales rep for Yellow Freight System for thirty years but I always had a greenhouse and growing rooms," he says happily.

For several years Harry operated Tadman's Florist and Greenhouses which included the garden center in his backyard and another one a short distance away. "I used to be the largest grower of orchids in Michigan. I had forty-five thousand square feet of glass for growing orchids and a big boiler for heating the greenhouses. It was another one of those things that I did in tens."

His face has brightened. His expressions become animated. He talks orchids with as much passion as he talked hosta. More than three thousand of the seven thousand known species of orchids are grown in greenhouses, he explains. The rest grow in tropical rain forests around the world. Harry Tadman knows this firsthand, because in the 1950s he forayed into the dense jungles of South and Central America and the West Indies in search of rare orchids. Such ventures were fraught with danger. Sometimes it was a toss-up as to which threat might be the worst. Venomous snakes? Poisonous insects? Contaminated water? Inhospitable natives? Uncooperative border guards?

"Me and my partner, a business man from Jackson, would make trips to Mexico. Anything you wanted in Mexico was just a matter of money. We made trips when we had guns pointed at us," he grins, never pausing to question what it was about orchids that made them worth risking their lives for.

Harry raised orchids until 1965, often barely able to meet the demand and always dispensing the same time-tested advice, "Keep the humidity up." He stopped raising orchids commercially after fire destroyed his boiler and some of the orchid houses, during weather that was twenty-one degrees below zero. His delicate orchid collection froze. He has replaced only a few favorite varieties.

It was when Harry was phasing out of the orchid business that he picked up a few hosta. They were, he says, just plants to add to his perennial gardens. That's all. Just a few plants. Then, somehow, a few became tens, and tens more tens, until they overtook him and empty greenhouses were once again bursting with new life.

But what is trying to overtake Harry now is ill health. He undergoes transfusions more and more often to build up blood weakened by a rare condition called *idio thrombopenia pupura*. His body is attacking its own good cells along with invaders, leaving him unable to fight illness. A treatment puts color in his cheeks, a glint in his eye, and a bit more pep to his step for a while, but not long enough to tackle the weeding in his flower beds he is itching to do.

His eyes narrow and his whole body tightens. There is no mistaking that what Harry Tadman is about to say matters enormously.

"I have wondered if all those years of handling insecticides has a lot to do with what has happened to both of us," he says, referring to his gardening buddy, Ted Kurnat. Ted, like Harry, came terrifyingly close to death, so close that his family was summoned to his bedside in intensive care. His liver was not functioning and his body was poisoning itself. At the eleventh hour, doctors landed on an antibiotic potion that worked and he pulled through. No one ever found a plausible explanation for what happened to cause his body to turn on itself much like Harry's. And, like Harry, Ted had liberally used chemicals in his earlier gardening days, to treat all kinds of plant ills. Both have quit using poisons entirely.

"I went to the specialists in Ann Arbor way back in 1970 when I started having problems," Harry says. His voice is edged with anger. "They asked me way back then if I used insecticides. I am against all of that stuff now. All of it."

His otherwise low-key demeanor remains hardened. "We humans are so smart we're dumb. We are killing ourselves through what we have done to our air, water, and food."

Harry would do something about what he sees happening around him if he were able. He would still like to be a biologist, a doctor, a deep sea diver, and a novelist. He has studied alternate theories on spirituality, past lives, and life forms in the universe and says with passion, "There is so much to learn."

Squirrels and chipmunks peer through the sliding glass door.

"I'm beginning to have a little more faith in people and in attempts to save nature," Harry says quietly as he watches a squirrel turn an acorn round and round between its paws. "I'd like for my grandchildren and my great grandchildren to be able to see things as I have because we cared enough to work to save nature."

For ever so brief a moment there isn't a sound as Harry surveys his gardens, ponds, and trees, his eyes tracing the curve of the trees' roots to the light playing on their uppermost branches. The birds are still. No breeze rustles through the leaves. For just this moment, all of nature, along with Harry, is sending silent prayers heavenward to a blue summer sky.

Message of the Autumn Leaf

My father loved the woods and all living things in it. Although he made a living for our family as a dairy farmer, his real love was working in the woods. The portion of our farm that was wooded represented a source of firewood, fence posts, and a few dollars from the sale of timber.

Months or even years in advance of the holidays he singled out evergreens that in due time would become our family's Christmas trees. Tromping out on a crisp pre-Christmas day to bring home that year's tree was a family ritual.

But the woods meant more to Dad than a source of goods or income. The woodland was also a place where Dad could retreat to find emotional refuge and spiritual renewal. He often said that he communed much better with his Maker while resting on a stump, watching the deer and squirrels, than he ever did sitting on a church pew.

Dad wasn't religious in the traditional sense of the word. He was spiritual, a man of quiet faith and selfless deeds. If a neighbor needed help, it didn't matter whether it was day or night or whether Dad was up to his elbows in his own work, he was there.

If one of us kids had a school play or a band concert, Dad was there.

When Mom was asked to take a leadership role with 4-H or Farm Bureau, he proudly supported her accomplishments.

And when he could stay awake long enough in the evening after barn chores were done, he read to my sisters and me from the *Moody Bible Story Book*.

When Dad no longer had the strength to keep the farm going and Mom's own struggles with arthritis were taking their toll, they sold the farm and with heavy hearts moved to town. Then, some years later, they left the community in which they had spent fifty-plus years of their lives to move closer to us – their daughters – who, by then like many farm kids, had gone away to college, marriage, and careers, never returning to farm life.

Mom and Dad moved to Battle Creek. They were just a few miles from the oncology center where he began receiving radiation therapy and were just three miles from my husband and me. On our ten acres outside the city, he and Mom could recapture the lifestyle most akin to that which they had known back in the Upper Peninsula. We had a couple of beef cattle, two horses, a cat and dog, and a large garden. To my parents, these were comforting reminders of home.

They drove to our place nearly every day, sometimes twice a day, to work in the garden and flower beds, and commune with the animals and nature, and were especially ecstatic when we purchased twenty-five acres of woods and wetlands which adjoined our original ten.

Wandering contentedly along the wetland, Mom could pick wild huckleberries and blueberries to her heart's content, while Dad dreamed aloud of cleaning out the underbrush, cutting neat riding trails, and of helping my husband put up firewood for the winter.

"Yup," he'd say, eyeing a section of the woods, "when I get to feelin' better I'm gonna work right over there."

His steadily declining health never allowed him to work there or any-where in the woods. He had to content himself with a bit of gardening, a lot of observing, and even more wishful thinking.

Every autumn, just as they had done when they lived in the Upper Peninsula, my parents took an annual "color tour." Dad marveled at the way in which what might have been a somber season of endings was transformed into a season of glorious transition through the majesty of the Creator's brilliantly-colored palette of golds, reds, orange, browns, and yellows.

On an exquisite day in October 1995, Mom and I took Dad to the oncology center where he received an injection of a long-acting painkiller, hoping to ease his discomfort in preparation for the holidays when the family would be together. He was weak, but tried to be of good cheer, joking with his oncologist as the medication was administered.

When his appointment was over, I pushed Dad's wheelchair to the car. As I opened the passenger door to help him get in, a huge, brilliant yellow maple leaf drifted down before him, settling gently at his feet. He pointed at it and smiled.

I bent to retrieve the leaf for Dad and looked for the tree which had nurtured such a perfect specimen. There were no maples close by. This magnificent leaf had somehow journeyed all the way across a parking lot to present itself to my father.

Dad was very tired but pleased when I offered to drive him and Mom out to a stretch of country road I knew was lined with especially beautiful yellow maples. During the drive he cradled the big leaf tenderly in his pale hands, turning it slowly by the stem as he admired the wonder of nature, and in little more than a wistful whisper expressed his awe and appreciation for God's handiwork and its meaning.

In its own wistful way the yellow leaf was telling Dad that the time had come for both of them to make a transition.

My father was gone not long after the last of the maple leaves drifted to the ground that year.

Several years have passed since Dad's death. The faded but still beautifully intact maple leaf graces my office, and in my front yard a maple tree has grown tall and stately. Every autumn it signals the changing seasons in brilliant yellow. Every autumn it reminds me that all of life is transition. All of life has a purpose. All is in the Creator's care and keeping, including my father.

* See also, "The Divine Touch," *Guideposts*, July 1996.

Soul Connection

Tyler Cappiello and his great grandfather, Ken Corey, shared a special bond. The two-year old loved to sit on "Big Papa's" lap, play with his cane, and eat whatever Big Papa was eating, especially strawberries.

No matter the pain Big Papa might be in from his advancing cancer, he pushed it aside when little Tyler came to visit. It seemed there was a soul connection that bridged the nearly eighty years between their ages.

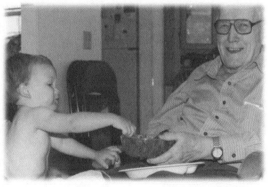
Tyler and Big Papa

Their time together was precious but too short. Tyler was not yet two and a half years old when Big Papa died just days before Christmas.

It would seem that a child so young would quickly forget an old man whom he'd known for such a short time, especially with all the excitement of the holiday season.

But not Tyler.

Soon after Christmas, as his parents whispered over early morning cups of coffee so as not to disturb their sleeping son, Tyler climbed out of bed and wandered into the kitchen.

"Did we wake you, honey?" his mom soothed, extending her arms to invite Tyler into her lap.

"Nuh uh," he murmured. "I have to tell you something."

"What do you want to tell us?" his dad asked.

"Big Papa is okay now."

"What was that?" his dad said, uncertain he had heard Tyler correctly.

"Big Papa is okay," Tyler repeated. "You should tell Great-Grandma."

Tyler's parents were incredulous.

"How do you know he is okay, honey?" they asked. "Did you have a dream about Big Papa?"

Tyler looked at one parent and then the other, and when he spoke his words were unmistakably clear.

"No, I didn't have a dream about Big Papa," he insisted. "We had a visit and he told me that. He said he is okay and for you to tell Great-Grandma."

Knowing that Big Papa was well and safe in heaven might have been all that was needed for Tyler to forget his Great-Grandpa Corey and get on with the business of being a growing boy. But as the years passed, time and again, his great grandfather slipped into his thoughts and conversations and even those of younger brothers, David and Brian, neither of whom had ever known Big Papa.

When Tyler learned to read he began asking first to hear and then to read for himself, the stories Big Papa had written about his life. The stories were Big Papa's legacy to his family of what life was like growing up on a farm in the early part of the twentieth century. They were stories of the land, hard work, and the sturdy family values that had guided his life.

Tyler was nine years old when just before Christmas 2002, his parents asked the three boys, as a part of their holiday preparations, to share the things they were thankful for. The boys' contributions were written on slips of paper and placed in a big bowl to be read a few at a time each night at dinner as Christmas drew near. Time and again as the slips were pulled from the bowl, there in Tyler's distinctive handwriting were the words, "Great-Grandpa Corey."

And now and then, when his parents come into his room to tuck him into bed they will find him embracing his pillow, staring sadly at the ceiling.

"I just miss Great-Grandpa," he says. "I just miss him."

The soul connection reaches across the years and as far as heaven is from earth, which isn't very far at all.

The Cottage from Hell

*There we stood, all four of us practically shoulder-to-shoulder ... all thinking
precisely the same thing, but not at that moment wanting to be the one to say it:
This is going to be the longest and worst week of my entire life.*

My husband had vacation time coming and we both knew that if we
stayed home we would spend the entire time working. We always do.
It's as if the lawn creeps up the windows and screeches, "Mow me!" The
weeds in the garden do multiplication tables overnight and the wood pile
threatens to disintegrate into compost if we don't split and stack it right
now.

Type A personalities. A blessing and a curse.

His eyes met mine with that I-know-what-you-are-thinking look.

"Let's go back to Rice Lake," he suggested.

"Sounds like a plan," I quickly agreed.

But this was already practically summer.

"Think we can find a place to stay this late into the season?" I asked,
fearing I already knew the answer.

"Dunno. All we can do is try."

Doyle checked the Internet for resorts on Rice Lake beginning with
the one we had enjoyed some fifteen years earlier. One by one we waded
through websites and placed calls only to be met with, "I'm sorry. No
vacancies." Not for two and surely not for four, since joining us on the
trip would be my mother and her friend, Lucille. The four of us made great
traveling companions.

After what seemed to be an exercise in futility, a resort owner offered a suggestion. "There's a place just down the road from us," she said hesitantly. "They might have something available."

There was something about the tone of her voice that gave pause for thought, but not for long. If we wanted to get away for a little R & R we might have to make do with just about anything – except a tent. With Mom in her eighties and Lucille close behind, roughing it was out of the question. We needed a real roof over our heads and something more than sleeping bags between us and the unyielding ground. How bad could it be at a lakeside resort? It was only for one little week.

We made the suggested call. A pleasant, gentle-voiced man answered the phone.

"Do you by any chance have any openings for the middle of July?" Doyle asked.

He had braced himself so much for "no," that he was caught completely by surprise when the answer was "yes."

"A cottage for four? You do?"

We were thrilled. The website images of a representative cottage showed the facilities to be spartan but adequate, and the price was right. Hurrah!

"Let's not expect too much," I cautioned amid our enthusiasm. "Looks can be deceiving."

* * * * *

It was a sweltering Saturday afternoon, when, after a ten-hour drive, we arrived at the resort neatly nestled between the lake and lovely rolling hills dotted with hayfields, cattle, and well-kept farms.

The view of Rice Lake as we crested the last of those hills was exquisite.

"Look at that, would you!" my mother chirped. "Oh, I am so happy we came!"

We were tired, ready for a good shower, a cold beer, a soothing rest, and, in due time, the gentle rocking of our fourteen-foot fishing boat instead of the *whrrr* of the van's wheels on pavement.

Quaint red cottages dotted the hillside as we drove onto the resort's grounds. A brand-new pool looked inviting and the grounds were neatly-kept.

"Your cottage is ready for you, yes?" the owner said, nodding cheerfully as he handed my husband a key at the office. We stepped out onto the porch and he motioned just across the driveway and a patch of lawn. "It is that one there. Called 'Bellaire,' yes?"

Our cottage, the only one not reserved when we had made our desperate call for a place to stay, was drab and box-like.

Doyle cast a sideways glance at me.

I shrugged.

We had purposely kept our expectations on the low side.

But not low enough.

The scrap of a weary old cottage was directly beside the circular gravel driveway that passed the office, the boat launch, continued on to the fish-cleaning shed, and looped past Bellaire's front door. The cottage rested on a concrete slab, and judging from the number of burrows dug under its foundation, we weren't the only tenants. The others, at least, had the benefit of cool shade. We certainly didn't. The cottage faced west with nary a tree between it and the lake, an open invitation for the intense afternoon mid-July sun to beat through threadbare curtains on tiny dingy windows.

"O-o-h gawd!" I gasped when we wrenched open the beaten-up door and stepped inside. "What in the world is that gawd-awful smell?"

The stench was such a dreadful combination of odors that our assaulted senses could barely sort them out.

"I think it's this soured rag mop," Lucille said, as she plucked a dirty bucket containing a gray sodden mop from a corner behind the table and hustled it outside.

The odor remained.

"It's probably the smell drifting this way from the fish-cleaning shed," Mom said, pulling back the curtain on the south window to note the shed just two buildings away. "We'll keep this window closed."

"Maybe it's something wrong with the pilot light on the heater or stove," my husband suggested, fiddling with the valve on the gas line. "Froze up," he said. "Can't do anything with it."

The stench was growing more offensive by the moment. My stomach churned. "There's got to be a dead mouse in here or something dead underneath this place," I insisted. "Maybe more than one. Maybe even the last people who stayed here."

There we stood, all four of us practically shoulder-to-shoulder in the Cottage from Hell, all thinking precisely the same thing but at that moment not wanting to be the one to say it. *This is going to be the longest and worst week of my entire life.*

We began struggling to open the tiny windows – except the one nearest the fish-cleaning shed – hoping to be saved by a breeze.

Mistake.

The proximity of our cottage to the office, boat launch, and main thoroughfare for the resort meant that every passing vehicle raised a powder-fine dust that drifted through the windows onto everything inside.

Not that it would have mattered.

The grimy at-one-time orange, paper-thin carpeting in the living room portion of the communal space served no useful purpose except to hide the rough, board flooring that rippled beneath it.

The carpeting was only a few dirty shades lighter than the sorry sofa against the north wall with a wobbly pressboard magazine table at each end. Those three pieces of furniture filled that entire wall of the cabin. The remaining scrap of space was taken up by a banged-up gas heater and a teeny tiny television on a broken stand. Lighting consisted of a very poor overhead fixture that cast a sickly greenish glow and a pair of scarred lamps with dull, yellow, rod-like bulbs under brittle shades.

"We'll bring in our camp chairs to have a place to sit other than just the couch," my mother offered, doing her best to think constructively. "That ought to work."

Her voice was artificially cheerful.

"But how can we arrange the chairs without bumping elbows or knees or blocking the door?" I asked.

If all four of us sat in the living room at one time we'd be shoulder-to-shoulder and knee-to-knee. There are limits to togetherness even among the best of friends.

She murmured something while Lucille, totally speechless, seemed to be searching, without much success, for something useful to add to the conversation.

The one-person kitchen space offered no encouragement. One person could open the fridge, use the sink, turn on the stove, and set the table all from the exact same spot. Mismatched faucets barely worked. Towel rods consisted of a rusty bar mounted under shabby cupboards, four nails above the stove, and a nail on either side of the door leading to the bathroom and bedrooms.

The oval dining table was covered by a red-checkered tablecloth – or at least it might have been red-checkered in a previous life. It was so faded that it no longer clashed with the mustard-yellow linoleum – where there was still linoleum.

The table stood on the highest point of the kitchen floor that sloped away in all directions, perhaps explaining why the refrigerator door had to be thumped shut with a foot each time it was opened.

From the tiny kitchen/dining/living area it was one step down (over the duct-tape covered copper pipes and wiring running along the step) to the bathroom on the left, a bedroom on the right and a bedroom immediately ahead, just past a door sill perfectly constructed to trip over in the night. One false step and the unlucky soul who went sprawling would clobber his head on that slight step up into the living "room."

"Mom and Lucille – you are not staying in that bedroom," I ordered protectively, pointing at the door sill in the narrow doorway. "We can't afford to have either one of you falling in the night and breaking in sixteen places. Doyle and I will take that room."

In the bedroom with the dangerous doorframe, the double bed took up all the space along two walls with the exception of a cubby-hole niche for a water heater near the foot of the bed. There was barely room to squeeze between the foot of the bed and the third wall. The last available space along the fourth wall, was occupied by a rickety old dresser and chair.

Mom and Lucille peeked warily into their assigned room, which, like the first, had two pillows and one blanket on a sagging double bed. At least the fragments on the beds appeared to have been blankets in an earlier incarnation. We breathed a collective sigh of relief that we'd brought our own bedding from home. The two people sleeping in that bed had better be on good terms because no matter which way they turned, without clinging to their respective edges of the mattress, they were going to end up wedged together in the middle.

There were no closets. Mom and Lucille had only a tiny dresser and a clothes rack that extended over the bed.

The bathroom was equipped with a toilet, miniscule sink, and a flimsy plastic shower stall so small that anyone of more than average proportions might be forced to come clean one side at a time.

There was no place to hang a towel – not so much as a nail sticking out of the wall – much less a towel rod, though the remains of a broken one lingered.

"Well ladies," Doyle announced as diplomatically as possible, "this is it. Our home away from home."

We began stoically hauling things into the cabin. A group of four or five men relaxing in lawn chairs in front of nearby cottages glanced our way now and then. They looked comfortable swilling beer in the cool shade of the lovely trees that surrounded their larger, neater cottages as we sweated our way back and forth between the van and the Cottage from Hell with our week's supply of food and gear.

With each necessity that we hauled inside, our premium space grew smaller as the men in the shade shook their heads and watched our every move. Was there something they knew that we didn't? Or, were they merely humored by the fact that while they had all left their wives behind, here was a good-hearted soul – or a darned fool – that not only had his wife along on a fishing trip, but his mother and maybe even mother-in-law besides?

The guy had to be a glutton for punishment!

We opened six of our seven windows, propped open the door, and set about consoling one another that once we got settled in, things would be better.

"We'll get the place aired out, spray some air freshener, spruce it up a little and it will be fine… just fine," Lucille assured me in her usual things-will-be-okay-way.

Mom dug right in with the cleanser and washcloths we had brought from home, scrubbing and washing the kitchen sink and table top. "We'll make it work," she promised.

The cheeriness in their voices had a hollow ring, but I had to give them credit for putting up a good front. If these gray-haired troopers could cope, well then, I darn well could too. This was our vacation, and vacations are supposed to be an adventure.

* * * * *

Adventure, yes. Exercise in self-punishment, no.

We sprayed the furniture, the bedding, the corners, the bathroom, and the kitchen with air freshener, grabbed snacks to eat in the boat, and headed out for an evening of fishing.

"It will be fine when we get back," Mom said. "We'll manage."

"Sure we will," Lucille echoed. "It will be fine...."

They must have been trying to convince themselves because they weren't convincing me.

Not our abundant catch or half a can of Lysol brightened my spirits or changed the appeal of the Cottage from Hell. As the sun dropped behind the islands in Rice Lake, my heart sank into the tennis shoes that by ten p.m. reeked from more than an hour in the scaly dampness of the fish-cleaning shed. Flies and mosquitoes clung to the screens, oogling us with beady little eyes and sharp incisors, waiting to torment our flesh, the moment the screen door was opened.

A shower, I wearily decided, would have to wait until morning.

I crawled into bed imagining what bloated, hairless carcass might be decaying under the floorboards beneath me. I tried to replace the image with visions of home-sweet-home which seemed oh so much sweeter by the moment and oh, so far away. But thoughts of home provided more regret than respite.

Despite the heavy humidity, with nary a breeze moving through the cabin, my husband fell asleep quickly, his snores having about the same volume and horsepower as the motor on our fishing boat.

The heat, his snoring, and the smell – all conspired to launch a massive assault on my senses. I buried my nose in the sweet freshness of my own precious blanket, comforted by the certainty that also having my own pillow meant there was nothing in it which might choose to crawl forth under cover of darkness and take up residence in my hair. The thought alone sent my scalp into a frenzy.

It took a very long time for me to fall asleep and I slept fitfully, taunted by visions of raccoon carcasses dancing with slimy fish wearing moldy mops on their heads.

* * * * *

It was around two a.m. when I jerked awake. It took no time at all to get my bearings. The room was hellishly hot, but hell would have been vastly better. There, at least, evil things burned. Here, they just rotted.

I felt my stomach beginning to do things that soon might add to the unpleasantness, especially if I tripped over the doorjamb before making it to the toilet.

While the others slept, I grabbed my pillow and the cottage's puny blanket from the foot of the bed and fumbled around until I located the keys to our van in the pocket of my husband's pants flung over the chair.

No one stirred.

I tiptoed to the front door, a big greenish yard light outside the utility building serving as my night light. No matter that I was wearing nothing more than one of my husband's t-shirts that barely covered matters of personal importance. I had to get out of that place – fast.

As quietly as possible, I slid open the side door of the van and climbed in, trying to remember what we had left in the back that I might have to climb over. I wanted to sleep lying down, not huddled in one of the front seats with the huge yard light beaming in my face.

I crawled between the seats and felt around the back of the van, finding enough room to weasel behind the back seats but in front of the spare tire, a tire iron, camp chairs, some plastic bags, and a tool box.

With the thin old blanket wrapped around the lower half of my body, my husband's blue jean jacket (a marvelous discovery) over my upper body, and the nylon boat tarp between me and the floor, I was as comfortable as I could ever hope to be. Cool and clammy as the floor of the van was, it smelled infinitely better than that miserable cottage.

Finally, I dropped off to sleep but woke and dozed, woke and dozed as the temperature dropped. It was not unbearable, but after a couple of hours I could no longer sleep. My hips and back ached.

As I stared into the shadows, a frightening thought crossed my mind. What if I did manage to fall asleep and was sleeping when daybreak came? There were many men staying here. Since a significant part of me was bare, there might be more naked to the visible eye than what I cared to reveal.

In addition to the guys staying in the cottage just across the way, any number of early-rising fishermen from other parts of the resort would be passing directly by our van on their way to the boat launch and docks.

The sight of a semi-naked woman sleeping with a trailer tire, tool box, and folding chairs might make for a topic of lively discussion.

"Hey Charlie, did you see what I saw in the back of that van?"

"Yah, wasn't sure if my eyes were playin' tricks on me or what after all that beer we put away last night. Whaddaya think is the story?"

"Dunno, but I'll betcha they had one helluva fight last night."

"Yah. Yer prob'ly right Joe. We shoulda told her she coulda come over to our cottage if she was that mad at him!"

"Did you get a good look at 'er? Not a chance!"

I had no interest in being any man's topic for discussion, particularly knowing how fishermen's stories have a tendency to grow into tales of unbelievable proportions.

But then, another equally vexing thought came to me. Suppose as daybreak came, the men were moving around. How would I get from the van back into the cottage and retain even a shred of dignity, wearing only my husband's t-shirt and a ragged yellow blanket?

How long could I wait to use a bathroom? I could just hear the men.

"Hey Charlie, lookit that woman climbing out of that van."

"Holy cow, look at 'er! Whaddaya think is the story?"

"Dunno, but I'll betcha he told 'er his wife is coming here later and he don't want the cabin smellin' like some other woman's perfume when she shows up."

"Yah. Yer prob'ly right. Darned poor of him to make her stay out there the whole blessed night with only that old blanket for cover. You'd think he coulda done something better for 'er than that. Cripes, I treat my gir..."

"You got a girlfriend Charlie? Why didn't you tell me? I thought we was buddies."

I shuddered. No way did I want to be cast in the role of some man's secret lover. And if that's what they imagined me to be, then dog-gone it, I ought to at least be a vision of loveliness with gorgeous hair and voluptuous curves accentuated by a tiny bright red teddy. Something that would, if nothing else, give these guys a much better place from which to start in concocting the stories they would certainly embellish when they got home. But I had neither gorgeous hair nor voluptuous curves, and I'd never worn a teddy in my life.

As quickly as these scenarios came and went, another much more horrifying possibility burst into mind. What if the problem in the Cottage from Hell really was the stove or heater and here I was, saving my own life while my husband, mother, and dear friend perished in their sleep? I had a responsibility to save them!

I stepped cautiously into the night chill. The coast was clear. Every cottage was dark and silent, including my own. The ground was cold under my bare feet, sending a shiver up my spine.

I pulled open the ill-fitting, clattery screen door as gently as I could, then leaned my shoulder against the equally ill-fitting wood door.

Errrch. Thunk. I was in. Snoring from both bedrooms reassured me that everyone was as wonderfully alive as the smell was grossly dead.

There was no point in turning on the overhead light to fumble my way to the couch. I didn't want to risk waking anyone and didn't want to be reminded of what the couch looked like anyway, knowing that I would have to put my nearly naked body against it. I could take comfort, at least, in knowing I was securely indoors and with the windows and door open, could get some cool night air. With any good fortune, air through the window just behind the couch would afford me some relief.

It didn't.

The pungent smell of fish remains wafted in on the night breeze. I pulled the neck of the t-shirt over my nose, and prayed I might awaken soon from what had to be a terrible nightmare.

* * * * *

As Sunday morning's golden light began to creep across the sky, I was still lying on the couch, still hoping for sleep and the end of the week. One by one my companions began to stir, trying to put on a cheerful façade.

"We'll have some breakfast, do some fishing, and maybe by then it will be better in this place," they suggested, as we bumped elbows, bottoms, and falsehoods, along with the refrigerator door.

"Okay," I moaned, "and while we're trying to make the best of things, let's all agree that the towel to dry the dishes hangs on the nail at the left corner of the doorway and the one to dry hands goes on the nail at the right."

"Good plan."

"Gotcha."

"What was that again? Dishes rights and hands left? Or was it the other way around?"

I wasn't sure.

Congratulating ourselves on having brought our own plates and plasticware from home, we had a spirit-lifting breakfast of fresh fruit, hot coffee, and sweet pastry.

Later, as we gathered poles and bait, tackle boxes and life jackets, to head out, we noticed something we had overlooked the evening before. Outdoors, along the north wall of the cottage directly under the window behind the couch, was a plastic recycle bin that someone had used not for bottles and cans but for fish entrails. The gray residue in the bin was gooey and gross.

Celebrating that maybe we had at last found the source of the foul odor, we quickly set the bin along the driveway to be taken away by the manager.

"Things ought to be better when we get back this time," Lucille said optimistically.

We trooped across the dusty driveway to our boat at the dock. Fishing had never been more appealing in my entire life than it was at that moment. Perhaps there was hope for this trip after all!

We were all nicely seated in the boat, preparing to ease out of the launching area, when I spoke up.

"Wait a minute," I said to my husband, motioning for him not to pull away from the dock. "Let me go to the office and see if they can get us into another cottage or check to see if there is a problem with the pilot light… just in case. If it isn't the pilot light, but a dead animal underneath the place… well… maybe they can remove it."

"Won't do any good," Doyle muttered, shaking his head. "We had trouble getting a place at all, remember? We got the last cottage. We'll just have to put up with it." He was itching to fish and was getting aggravated with me.

"Just let me try," I fussed.

If there was anything my husband of nearly twenty-six years knew about me, it was that I am outspoken about things that matter, and this mattered. If there was a prayer's chance something could be changed, I had to give it my best shot. How many nights could I sleep in the van?

"I don't think there's anything we can do," he shrugged again. "Go talk to the owner anyway if it will make you happy. But hurry up."

I trotted into the office where the slight-of-build man smiled at me from behind the registration desk. He listened attentively as I explained our dilemma with the cottage, the possibility that the source of the stench might be a problem with the pilot light, or worse. I even told him with as much good humor as I could muster, that I had tried to sleep in our van.

"I am sorry!" he said, perhaps a bit too knowingly. "You are in the cottage we call 'Bellaire', yes?" He turned to reach up to rows of keys hanging from small nails, plopped a key in my hand, and said, "I have another cottage I can offer you, yes? We had a no-show that was supposed to come same time as you. You can have Akron Cottage if you wish." He was eager to make us happy.

Relief and hope washed over me. "May we take a look at it?" I asked excitedly, thinking that to be a much more politically-correct response than, "Mind if we smell it?"

"Certainly," he said, nodding vigorously as he described how I should follow the boardwalk from the office, head north along the waterfront, and when the boardwalk ended at its northern-most point, Akron would be the cottage beside the little cove.

When I came out of the office, gleefully waving a key, Lucille climbed from the boat. We hustled down the boardwalk, hardly daring to hope that we might find a cottage much more to our liking, or if not to our liking at least to our level of tolerance.

One by one we passed nice cottages, almost afraid of what we might find at the end of the boardwalk. We turned right beside a nice wooden bench that faced the water and there it was. A lovely little place facing the cove! Akron Cottage.

* * * * *

The cottage was surrounded by lovely big trees, had its own little front yard facing the lake, and was well away from the main drive onto the resort's grounds.

The outdoor light over the small entryway to the cottage was covered with layers of cobwebs and tree debris as we stepped onto a small stoop. Maybe this cottage was not occupied for a reason other than a no-show?

Lucille looked at me. I looked at Lucille.

"Ready?" I asked.

"Ready," she said. "Go for it."

Hesitantly we unlocked the door and stepped inside. Every nerve ending in my nose was on full alert.

Voila!

The smell alone was nasal bliss and there was room to move. In comparison to Bellaire, Akron Cottage was paradise! Without seeing another feature I knew we had been saved, but it got better from there. The kitchen area was neat, and was at the opposite end of a long narrow room, probably ten by twenty-four. The room comfortably contained a weary but still serviceable couch, a good-sized dining table with four chairs, and a bank of windows facing the little yard and lake. We had an easy chair, a good television tucked neatly in a corner, and a nice gas heater.

"Oh-h check this out!" Lucille cooed from one of the two bedrooms. She had climbed up a little ladder to plop on a bunk bed. "Ah," she said, sprawling out and wiggling first one way and then the other. "This feels good. I can sleep here just fine!"

At seventy-eight she had all the child-like enthusiasm of an eight-year old!

I peeked into the other bedroom. The bed was big, firm, and neat. Although there were still no closets, the walls were lined with hooks and generously supplied with hangers. There were narrow but good-sized, curtained windows in both rooms.

We found still more things to celebrate – a new sink with good faucets in the kitchen space, a nice countertop for meal preparation, and a big window right beside the stove to deliver a cool breeze off the lake. There was even a clean refrigerator in excellent condition and good cupboards!

The linoleum too, was amazingly beautiful compared to what we'd found in the Cottage from Hell. It was a cream-color with a soft gold diamond pattern here and there. There were wood floors in the bedrooms, antique dressers, and nary a scrap of ancient carpeting in the place. Ah, how grand.

The bathroom was only a tiny bit larger than that in the first cottage but had a window over the toilet that could be left open for a refreshing cool breeze. The shower stall and sink were in good repair.

Behind our sturdy entry door was a shelf for our fishing hats, and beneath it, hooks for jackets– a simple little feature too wonderful for words.

"Can you believe this place?" I sang.

To our enormous delight, our little yard had mature trees to give refreshing shade from the afternoon sun (a clothesline was already strung between two of them), and we had our very own picnic table!

A split-rail fence and more trees along the north side of the cottage marked the end of the resort's property. There was no dust, no driveway, no blazing sun. Lucille and I were nearly beside ourselves with delight.

"Oh," she said again and again. "This will work just fine. Just fine!"

We hurried back to the office, worried that in the intervening minutes between being offered this magnificent specimen and having given it a look/smell, the rightful renters might have shown up to stake their claim. I was already steeling myself to protect our new turf.

The owner again smiled broadly as I came through the office door. He knew our answer before I gave it. "You like it, yes?" he asked, though our faces did the answering.

"We will take it!" Lucille and I chimed.

"You don't have to move your things right now," he beamed. "Go fishing. Have a good morning. I can help you later."

Hugging him would probably have been a little more 'thank you' than what the occasion warranted, but I was certainly tempted.

He winked.

* * * * *

After a wonderfully successful morning landing a generous measure of bluegill, perch, and sunfish, we returned to Akron Cottage, mooring our boat at our own sturdy dock beside the lovely bench just feet away from our cabin. If we had been pulling a million dollar yacht into a marina in front of our own condo, we couldn't have felt any better.

We studied the cottage as we climbed from the boat. Was anyone

sixty-six, designed the one-floor, open concept home for her and Ray's retirement years.

sixty-eight, bought her first four-wheeler for getting around the tree farm.

sixty-nine, with Ray, made the first of eleven driving trips to Tampa, Florida, at three thousand two hundred miles a trip.

seventy-two, got her first traffic ticket (and says slyly, "They've only managed to catch me one time since").

seventy-five, quit a twenty-year job shearing Christmas trees, figuring "that was enough."

seventy-eight, bought her first VCR and video camera.

eighty, climbed the TV antenna tower to place a lighted Christmas tree at the top.

eighty-one, got her first computer and began recording family history.

eighty-four, got her second computer, a newer genealogy program, and began tracking her stock holdings. "I check on the market several times a day," she admits, "to see whether I am gaining or losing."

eighty-five, served as executrix of her sister's estate.

eighty-six, was one of the first people in her rural area to get an e-mail address.

eighty-eight, became e-mail grandma to a class of third graders.

eighty-nine, appeared in a "Mrs. Senior Michigan Pageant" and was, to no one's surprise, its oldest contestant. While younger entrants in the competition chose musical talent to demonstrate their

Ethel at play

suitability for the title, Scotty chose to list her talents as having a good command of the English language and possessing good listening skills. Apparently those weren't quite the attributes the judges were looking for. Even wearing one of her "enhanced" bras was not enough to capture the title.

Also at the age of eighty-nine, when most gray-haired ladies want to take things a bit slower or may not be moving much at all, Scotty bought her third new computer – one that would work faster.

"This one has Solitaire," she says. "I play that to overcome the stress I feel when I don't win at the casino." She takes the bus with other senior citizens to the Indian casino in Harris two or three times a week. She keeps an accounting of her wins and losses and has done right well for herself.

People have different ways of relieving stress, even people who have passed the age of ninety. Solitaire may be one, but Scotty's usual means of finding contentment in the summertime, is to mow the five acres of grass around her big yard, edged with apple trees, evergreens, and hardwoods.

But in the winter she has to find another way to burn off energy, so she hauls out the snow blower and cleans the driveway. Long Upper Michigan winters generally provide an adequate supply of the white stuff right into April.

A feature story about Ethel Casimir in the *Escanaba Daily Press*, dated January 13, 2001, showed her trucking along behind a snow blower three times her size. Wrote the reporter, "…when you spot her, you immediately

realize that the snow blower isn't the huge monstrosity you initially thought it to be… its pint-size operator is scarcely five feet tall." The article was titled, "Pint-size Dynamo Keeps Going and Going and Going…."

The many chores Scotty has tackled alone, Ray would have done had he been able. If anyone knew how to work and work hard, it was Ray. Even into his early nineties he stayed busy around their cozy home. But the Alzheimer's

Ethel at work
Photo: *Escanaba Daily Press*

stole away his ability to

remember how to do the things he loved, even if his body was still willing to do them. He was nearing his ninety-fifth birthday when Scotty finally could no longer take care of him at home. Although slight of build, he was too heavy for someone five-foot-nothing to handle. If he fell, getting him to his feet was a struggle. And too, the gravel road runs very close to their front yard, so if Scotty wasn't there to watch him every moment, he could easily have wandered into the path of a vehicle. The very thought twisted her nerves into knots. Reluctantly, only because there was no other alternative, Scotty placed Ray in the only nursing home nearby, which, fortunately, was just seven miles from their home. Ironically, it was the same facility where she had once been confined for tuberculosis and had later worked as a nurse.

Every day, no matter the weather, Scotty made the drive to the home to feed Ray. Only a dozen times in the two years he was there, and then only because of bad weather, was Scotty not at his bedside at least once a day.

Although the Alzheimer's disease caused this once gentle, kind-spirited man to begin refusing to eat, Scotty still coaxed him to open his mouth, one spoon, one sip at a time. Day after day she cajoled. Day after day she still loved and when he passed away she was at his side.

Life goes on and Scotty does too. She's no quitter. She's taken a couple of rough spills on the ice in her yard in recent years. "I fell flat on my nose one time," she says, chuckling about it in retrospect. "My two black eyes and scabby nose turned yellow. You'd think I had been in a bar-room brawl, but honestly, I only went out to get the mail!"

Upper Michigan winters that can turn roads to sheets of ice for days at a stretch made it a relief, to a degree, when Scotty no longer had to make the nursing home trips each day. "But that is no compensation for being without the one you love, and with whom you've shared sixty years," she says. From her living room windows she can watch her menagerie of birds and squirrels dine at several feeders. Deer, rabbits, and other critters from the Michigan woods know they have a friend in Scotty Casimir. That is, of course, except during gardening season when she'd much prefer to enjoy at her own table, the vegetables and fruit the critters have eagerly been watching ripen, certain that these delicacies were planted just for them.

It's a different world now, and yet the same. It is different because

Ray is gone as is their old dog Smokey, a good buddy especially after Ray was in the nursing home. But, it's the same world too, because it is still the same home where Scotty keeps company with her wild critters and a world that has expanded with the technology of e-mail.

Scotty's role as an e-mail grandma began entirely serendipitously.

"My granddaughter, who taught in the Fort Wayne, Indiana school, was writing an e-mail to me one day from her classroom while the children were busy, and had begun it as 'Dear Grams,'" Scotty explains. "One of her students happened to see it and asked if she could send Grams a note too."

The correspondence quickly spread across the classroom. The children were captivated with the notion that somewhere out there was a real live grandma they could adopt as their own, write to any time they wanted, and best of all, could hear from every single day. E-mailing became a wonderful way for them to practice their letter-writing, spelling, grammar, and computer skills without even remotely considering these things as school work.

During the nearly two years of correspondence, Scotty neatly slipped in lessons in history, geography, science, and citizenship as she shared her life with her young friends, telling them about places in the world, the wildlife in her backyard, and the joy the animals bring her as well as the ways that people should treat the creatures of the earth and be kind to one another. Her letters to them were warm and filled with wonderful things that caught their interest and sparked in them a curiosity to learn more.

Scotty's first letter to the children began at the beginning....

"I was born in 1910 in Manistique Michigan, on Cedar Street, at the home of my parents...."

A poster soon graced the wall behind the teacher's computer with pictures of Scotty, her home, the little dog Smokey, and some of the animals she feeds. Most of Scotty's young friends live in apartments or houses within congested neighborhoods of the city. They had little comprehension of what it is like to live near the woods or among wild animals that become friends.

The city kids were fascinated by the beauty of Scotty's rural surroundings on a hill that overlooks woods, intersected by a gravel road and dotted with fields, fences, and farms. They were especially intrigued by the rickety picnic table at the edge of the woods behind their e-mail Gram's house. There, she spreads a daily buffet of sunflower seeds, bread crumbs, suet, and other delicacies for her wild family.

Scotty's cluttered little computer/office nook in a room off her bedroom is a treasure-trove of memorabilia from "her kids." Photographs of each and every child are tacked to the wall and an ever-growing file of both e-mail and handwritten letters spills over from the desk to another table. She has saved every letter, and responded to every child personally, sometimes writing three and four short, but personal, letters each day.

E-mail Grams and the children exchanged videos and gifts too. One winter each of the children made a pine cone/peanut butter/bird seed bird feeder for E-mail Grams to hang in her yard, and as Scotty opened their gifts, her daughter-in-law captured the magic of the moment on videotape. The children, seeing the video back in Fort Wayne, were entranced by the happiness they had brought to "their" grandma.

Dear Grandma,

I went to Michagan before. Have you went Califorena?
I lived there for 5 years. I wish you could come for Christmas.
P.S. I wish you could be my Grandma.
Your friend,
Jennifer

Dear Jennifer:

No, I have never been to California except to fly over it when my husband and I went to Hawaii 25 years ago on our 35th wedding anniversary. I don't think I could come for Christmas as all my children, grandchildren, and great- grandchildren will be here that day.

Your friend, E-Mail Grandma

Dear Grandma,
How are you? I am sorry your dog died.
At least you still have us. We know how you feel our hamster died.
> Your friend,
> Codi

Dear Codi:
I am OK, and very happy to have you and your class-
mates to write to. It is like summer here today and
I should be outside putting food on the table for the
birds and deer. They will be here soon. Am sending
you a picture of one of my visitors.
> *Your E-Mail Grandma*

"I got such a nice video from my kids," she says reflecting on her e-mail experience. "They were dancing and singing and looked so happy. In my thank you letter I told them how much I enjoyed it and that when I was in the third grade we didn't have radios, TV, video cameras, and computers, or, of course, e-mail. At that time there were only a few cars and even fewer airplanes. How lucky these kids are. I wonder what miracles the next twenty years will bring?"

The next twenty years will bring many changes, some of which will likely help the children and others which will not – too many cars, too many airplanes, too much congestion, and too few connections to the woods and wild creatures. In her own way E-mail Grams has given these youngsters an opportunity to feel the spirit-filling wonder, delight, and satisfaction that comes from living in harmony with nature.

"E-mail Grams," many of the letters began or ended, "You are the best Grams/friend I have ever had...."

Scotty is a friend because she listens, she praises, she gives advice when it is sought, and she has allowed the children into her world at their own request. They have learned about her years as a nurse and that at one time in her younger years she earned only six dollars for twenty hours of work. That gives real substance for a math lesson and appreciation of an allowance. They knew from what she said in her e-mails that she has been a newspaper reporter and a community volunteer. E-mail Grams taught the children the meaning of volunteerism in a way that makes them want to do nice things for other people too. She told them that she sometimes reads several books a day which is one of the reasons she has so many interesting things to share. They learned how and why it is that her garden grows so beautifully, and have learned from her example that healthy exercise outdoors is good for the body and the soul.

Although Scotty is no longer an e-mail grandma to an entire classroom of children, she is still writing her life's story. She no longer worries that she needs to do it because her children will never get to see her grow old. Just before her 90th birthday in 2000, she wrote:

Care Enough to Share

For inner tranquility, I have found that sharing has always brought a feeling that is pleasing to remember. Care enough to share the bounty of your garden, whether it is those first two tomatoes or the surplus of beans, zucchini, squash, and cucumbers. Share the fruit from your orchard, the flowers from your colorful display, or even your dreams and thoughts. They all might make a difference to someone when you care enough to share.

And even more recently she wrote a piece that challenges the reader to consider his or her own attitude toward life:

When you see an older person, do you look at their wrinkles, sagging chin, and pot belly, or do you see their twinkling eyes and happy smile?

Do you send your mother a beautiful bouquet of flowers for her to enjoy, or, do you intend to wait until she dies and send them to the funeral home?

Your attitude toward life is the difference between a happy, congenial personality or a grouchy, complaining nincompoop. Which are you?

Scotty Casimir doesn't have time to be a nincompoop, even if she knew how to be one.

There's a bingo game to be played and it's time to get going.

There are choices to be made about what to wear. Part of her wardrobe, after all, is hanging on a doorknob.

Life is full of some big — and even bigger decisions.

Just Call Me Russ

"A shirtsleeve executive is what I've been called and I take it as a compliment.
I have certain values that I believe are right.
There is no discontinuity between who I am and what I do."
-Russ Mawby

A college professor, new to the faculty at Battle Creek's Kellogg Community College had moved to nearby Augusta. It was picturesque rural property, especially because, among his new neighbors were several with manes and tails. He envied the way the animals could spend their days contentedly grazing or standing in the shade. It became a habit to look for the horses, ponies, and miniature donkey before he left for work, and again when he returned home.

On one particular afternoon, however, he glanced out his window to find that a few ponies had gotten out of their pasture and had wandered into another neighbor's yard. Fortunately, someone was already tending to the escapees.

The professor, thinking this was a good opportunity to get acquainted, set out down the farm lane between the properties. A middle-aged man dressed in a faded denim jacket and dirt-smudged overalls, was helping a woman coax her ponies through a gate back into their own pasture. Loose threads hung from the elbows of the man's jacket where it had been torn in several places from many years of farm labor. Splotches of paint here and there added a touch of character. His scuffed boots were obviously well-acquainted with the good earth.

The professor studied the man as he approached. *Poor fellow*, he thought. *He's had a tough go of it but he certainly looks like a hard worker.*

"Hello there!" he called out from several feet away.

The workman was bent over, a wire staple or two tucked between his lips, while with one hand he held a staple over a bit of loose fencing wire, and with the other wielded a hammer.

"I saw you tending to the ponies and thought I would introduce myself. I'm the Mawby's new neighbor." The professor motioned back across the meadow to point out his house.

The fence the workman was repairing, adjoined the farm belonging to Dr. Russell G. Mawby, chief executive officer of the W. K. Kellogg Foundation, which is one of the world's largest philanthropic organizations. Dr. Mawby was known and respected throughout the world. An average day might find him meeting with university presidents to discuss issues in academia, delivering a keynote address to health professionals, visiting the barrios in Latin America to better understand the needs of society's overlooked populations, or accepting yet another prestigious honor.

The worker pulled off a worn glove and extended his hand across the fence, a broad smile breaking across his face as he plucked the staples from his mouth.

"Hello!" he replied in a deep resonant voice as he pushed his cap back from his forehead.

As the two men shook hands, the professor offered an introduction. "I've just joined the faculty of Kellogg Community College," he said. "You must be..." he paused, "the Mawbys' hired man?"

The workman smiled a warm smile. "Russ Mawby," he said with a firm handshake and a twinkle in his eye, "Just call me Russ!"

* * * * *

So goes a story that has circulated for many years in many circles about Dr. Russell G. Mawby, a man unlike many of his peers in the academic, high-powered, and sometimes elitist world of philanthropy. It is a story repeated with admiration for a person who might have chosen to fit in, but opted instead to remain true to himself and his core values. He has been called the "shirtsleeve executive" and takes no offense at the moniker, though at the helm of a six billion-dollar organization he could have demanded to be called most anything.

Another popular (and also true) story about Russ, as he really does prefer to be called, relates that a Bicentennial parade was being held at the Detroit State Fair. There were the usual tissue-paper floats, children on decorated bicycles, old cars, prancing horses, fire trucks with flashing lights, organizations touting their causes, antique putt-putt tractors, and flag-waving politicians. But people along this parade route took note of something unusual, a suspendered fellow in work pants, a faded plaid shirt, a black felt hat, and farm boots, strolling easily beside a team of yoked oxen. The brown and white beasts ambled along, pulling a big-wheeled ox cart, as children not at all accustomed to seeing such lumbering one-ton animals, squealed from the sidewalks.

One of the oxen, slowing to do what all oxen need frequently to do (more so it seems during parades on clean city streets), lifted its tail to leave a business card. Immediately, the oxen driver brought the team to a stop, pulled a shovel from his cart and scraped up the steamy pile before continuing on.

A parade-watcher along the sidelines turned to his companion, pointed at the oxen driver and gasped in amazement, "Can you believe it? I read in the paper only this morning that he – that man right there – just gave away ten million dollars!"

Well of course Russ Mawby hadn't personally given away that amount of money, but philanthropic grants made by the Kellogg Foundation under his leadership and the guidance of the Foundation's board of trustees, at times were that large and larger. The Foundation's purpose in grant-making is to use the earnings from its assets and investments to improve human well-being. It does that by making grants across the U.S. and world to improve health care, education, leadership, and agricultural practices.

Over the course of Russ Mawby's thirty-one years with the Foundation (1964 -1995), its assets, a large portion of which came from stock in the world-famous Kellogg cereal company, grew from roughly $364 million to more than $6.45 billion, making it second in size at that time only to the Ford Foundation. During those years, Russ was keenly involved in decision making, which allocated more than $2.5 billion to hundreds of projects.

Grantmaking is a role for which Russ Mawby is well-suited because he loves people, loves to see good things happen for people, and as anyone who knows him can tell you, many of the dozens upon dozens of speeches he has delivered all over the world end with the words, "In the final analysis, only people matter. Only people are important."

But who would ever associate the highest ranking officer in such an important and influential organization with common farm labor, oxen driving, or pooper-scooping?

Only those who know Russ Mawby.

Dr. Mawby... Russ... is not your ordinary executive, especially not in these days of executive chicanery. Now that he is retired – although one look at his appointment calendar would raise some doubt about that – he reminisces with wistfulness and contentedness about the reasons why he has enjoyed such a successful career.

Consider, for example, that this man, who has held several highly-sought-after positions, has never applied for a job in his life. Or that his granddaughter says he's "a little weird," not because he talks to his animals but because he thinks they talk back. (One of his closest confidants is Sí Señor, a quite senior, miniature Mediterranean donkey, who, according to Russ, does not like to be asked his age.) Or that as a part-owner of a few Standardbred racing horses, he confesses to having consistently owned the half that crosses the finish line last.

"The end that crosses the finish line first earns the roses," says his long-time friend and co-race horse owner, Pres Kool, "The other end feeds 'em." Both men delight in reciting a favorite line – "We sold one of our race horses to an Amish couple to use as a buggy horse. We got a letter the other day saying they had been late to church three Sundays in a row!"

Russ Mawby holds the distinction of having been the only person to drive a team of oxen (Yankee and Doodle) down Constitution Avenue in Washington, D.C., for the nation's Bicentennial parade. He is also most likely the only CEO of any organization to have farm animals present at his retirement party, or to host an "open barn party" in a horse's honor. (Where are the tabloid reporters when you need them?)

But true confessions don't stop there.

It's no exaggeration to say that there are a large number of highly educated people who dish out a lot of "BS," but how many would actually say so on a business card?

Russ Mawby would. And did.

This man, who holds a Ph.D. and nineteen honorary doctorates, at one time actually had a business card that read, "BS Incorporated. Service Is

Our Business." While it is true that the pursuit of a B.S. may require learning a lot of BS, the letters in this usage stood for "Bull Syndicate." Russ was co-owner of a bull available for... well... syndication.

Based on that business venture, one would wonder how he ever succeeded in the highly competitive business world, because he admits that he and his syndication partner, Maurice Seay, "had an image problem." People, he says, feigning surprise, just didn't realize what the BS really signified.

Everything about Russ Mawby's position and the respect he has achieved in so many prestigious places, says he should be living in the "right" neighborhood, belonging to the "right" church, traveling in the "right" circles, and holding membership in the "right" country club where he seals major deals with the shake of a hand and the swing of a golf club.

And he does. He lives in the neighborhood that is exactly right for the lifestyle that he loves with a passion, and is just down the road from the country church where he is a familiar face. He travels in the "circles" that are right for him and even better for his harness horses. The country is all the country club he needs and he plays golf regularly – one time a year for a charity fundraiser.

No matter whether he shakes your hand across an executive desk or a farm gate, he stands behind his word. Whether in the workplace or work boots, Russ Mawby is the same person with a consistency and genuineness that is increasingly rare these days.

The facets of Russ Mawby's life are many and varied. He has been 4-H agent and university professor, foundation executive and community leader, philanthropist and fruit farmer, race horse owner and oxen driver. He is husband, father, grandpa, and neighbor. He has dined with world leaders at palatial estates and exchanged "howdies" with the folks who happen to be sitting at the next booth at the modest little Hickory Inn in tiny Hickory Corners, Michigan. (The eatery with all the pickup trucks parked out front.)

Russ has rested suited elbows on a finely finished mahogany table surrounded by corporate dignitaries, and has leaned faded shirtsleeves atop a rough board fence to watch his horses graze. He is awed more by a night sky than by the fact that he has trice been knighted (Norway,

Denmark, and Finland). He is more content munching sandwiches with youngsters in a 4-H Club than he is sampling hors d'oeuvres at a country club. He prefers a whiffletree to a golf tee.

Russ Mawby retired from his Kellogg Foundation leadership role in 1995 but remains an honorary and dedicated member of its board of trustees. He lives in the same home on the same farm where he has lived for more than forty years.

When Ruth, his wife of fifty years, became ill from the complications of post-polio syndrome and diabetes in the early 1990s, he began to ease out of many leadership roles. After her death in May of 2000, his own health challenges necessitated that he curtail involvement even more. Still, the positive attitude for which he is well known remains evident, as does his enthusiasm for helping humankind.

It was Russ Mawby who signed my first 4-H club certificates in 1964 when I was nine years old and he was Michigan's Director of 4-H Programs. It was he who approved my hiring at the Kellogg Foundation some sixteen years later. His face lit up when he scanned my résumé.

"Can you remember the 4-H pledge?" he asked.

"I pledge my head to clearer thinking, my heart to greater loyalty...." I began.

He never stopped smiling as I recited the entire pledge, then he nodded approvingly.

Over the next decade, as a communications and evaluation professional, I would have the opportunity to observe him in many venues at the Foundation and to work directly with him on occasion, but most importantly, to know him as a dear friend in the years that have followed.

One summer afternoon in 2002, we visited as we do from time to time over tall glasses of lemonade in his comfortable living room. On the wall behind him was a large oil painting done by a family member, depicting a boy strolling along a country road shaded by towering maples. On another wall, a set of four prints of stately barns accented an antique whiffletree, beside a stone-age axe presented to him by the Danish Smallholder's Association. In another area, a silhouette carefully cut from aged, gray barn wood, of the head of a draft horse, adorned with a leather bridle, was mounted to a stone fireplace. Nothing formal and stuffy. Everything warm and welcoming.

We chatted and chuckled about shared interests: 4-H and horses, farms and the out-of-doors. We joked about the race horses I once boarded for him and the humorous, witty letters "they" wrote me after they moved on in their careers; letters whose hoof-writing was remarkably similar to Russ' handwriting. I asked him to tell me about his growing-up years, ever fascinated with how he acquired the values that have guided his life.

"Did I ever tell you that I was named for my grandfather, Remus G. Mawby?" he began. "He was an English immigrant who came to this country as a teenager in the 1880s and ended up on a little fruit farm in Plainfield Township, northeast of Grand Rapids. My folks changed Remus to Russell. I'm grateful for that for some reason!" His eyes crinkled at the corners.

Russ' parents, Wesley and Ruby, attended the one-room Peach Grove School in that little farming neighborhood, completing their formal education in the eighth grade, which was all the schooling available to them at the turn of the last century. His father went to work for Oscar Braman, a successful Grand Rapids-area fruit farmer.

"Oscar was an innovator in fruit production and management, and he encouraged my dad to go to a fruit-growing short course at Michigan Agricultural College in East Lansing," Russ remembers. "Dad took the train to Lansing in 1913, walked to East Lansing, and took the classes that changed his future dramatically. He and my mother got married and in 1925 bought one of Oscar Braman's farms, the one hundred-forty acres that became the Mawby farm where I was born and raised."

With his three siblings, Russ who was born in 1928, attended the Orchard View School, a two-room country school on the corner of his family's farm. First through fourth grades were in one room and fifth through eighth in the other, with two teachers and the older students to help the younger ones along.

"That was progressive education," he says with a grin, "way back when."

It is apparent both in Russ' tone of voice and body language that he holds his parents in high regard as he recalls them and the values they imparted.

"My folks, while not having much in the way of credentialed education, were lifelong learners. Dad was involved in cooperative extension programs and worked closely with the researchers in the horticulture department at the Agricultural College which later became Michigan State University (MSU). He served on the Michigan State Apple Commission and was what rural sociologists call an 'early adopter.' He experimented with adopting new technology to fruit-growing, including being one of the first fruit farmers to build an apple storage building."

In the early 1900s until about the 1940s, apples were often stored in the basement portions of converted barns. When a farmer no longer kept dairy cattle, the stanchions were torn out and the windows were boarded up to keep the area as cool as possible for apples but not always with great success. The Mawby's specially-designed apple storage building was built partially underground of cement and was air-cooled by huge chunks of ice placed in ice bunkers. Later, refrigeration replaced the ice, to preserve the apples at a constant temperature year-round.

But Wes Mawby's adopter skills did not stop there. He took on the grocery business. In the early days of grocery shopping, a shopper stepped up to a wooden counter behind which the clerk waited to fill orders. The clerk was handed a list and scurried about, gathering cans of this and scoops of that from bulk containers, weighing items himself, one at a time. But the day came when grocers no longer found it practical to work that way. They wanted goods in containers that the shopper could self-select.

"My dad was one of the first to prepackage apples into five-pound mesh bags that were dyed purple to accentuate the color of the apple," Russ notes. "There were six bags to a standard crate and one of Dad's first customers was a gentleman named Frederik Meijer. Mr. Meijer's first store was at the north edge of Greenville, Michigan. I used to deliver bagged apples to him for my father."

The success of the first Meijer store led to another in Ionia and then a third in Grand Rapids. That was the beginning of the Meijer multi-million dollar, mega-store enterprise.

Wesley Mawby's entrepreneurship did not stop with growing, storing, packaging and delivering apples. He also distributed insecticides and fungicides for orchard spraying. Russ remembers traveling to other orchards with his father and listening while he explained how to properly mix and apply the chemicals.

By process of observation and participation, the younger Mawby learned to communicate effectively, work responsibly, and manage efficiently. The learning occurred with his mother's help as well. At a time when careers were off-limits to many women, Russ Mawby's mother was active in homemaker extension work and was a volunteer 4-H leader. He saw firsthand how couples should work as a team for the success of the enterprise.

"We were continually engaged with the extension service, the county agricultural agent, the 4-H leader, and the home demonstration agent," Russ remembers. "We were active in 4-H. These people were part of our lives, and so it was just assumed that we would follow. My older brother went to agricultural short course to continue the fruit-growing tradition in our family, and my sister went to a two-year college. I was the first to earn a four-year baccalaureate degree with 4-H scholarships that totaled almost one thousand dollars over the four years I was at Michigan State University."

That level of scholarship support was extraordinary for the times. Russ' younger brother also later earned a bachelor's degree from MSU.

In addition to the Mawby family's extension connections, Russ' parents were very active in Red Cross drives, the United Way fund drives, and other aspects of civic life.

"A lot of my values came from those experiences as a kid," he affirms. "What's important, too, is that we were not exploited as children on the farm but were part of the labor force. I was not athletic in high school, so I would come right home rather than be involved in sports. In the fall, the apples would have been picked by our workers all day, so that when I got home, I drove tractor and we'd haul apples to the apple building 'til eight-thirty at night, then go get ice for the ice bunkers. In those working relationships you learned a lot of values of work, cooperation, responsibility."

Russ leans back against the sofa to rest. He has to be careful or a painful hip begins to complain. Outside, cardinals, wrens, and sparrows chatter and flit from feeder to feeder and from limb to limb in pines, maples, oaks, and evergreens.

He eases into some of the stories from his youth and his years as a rapidly-rising young professional, talking easily without pretense or self-importance about the values that mean so much to him. Those values have a way of becoming even more important as time gets away and the people who taught them are no longer around. We have a responsibility, he says, to teach them to the generations who follow.

"Funny how you remember a lot of incidents that stick with you...," he continues, glancing up at one of the rural farm images on the wall as if stepping into the scene and back in time.

Do an honest day's work. "I remember my father's uncle John. He worked for Dad and was in his late sixties or seventies. John at one time had a small fruit farm and had retired over in the North Park area outside Grand Rapids. He worked part-time for Dad after he retired. He could trim trees, thin peaches, and help do a lot of things. Uncle John had a beautiful old Model T Ford that he kept spotless. He would drive it out to our farm and park it on the shady side of the shed so that it would stay cool, and would cover each of the tires with a burlap bag so they wouldn't get too much sunlight."

Russ gestures, imaginary burlap in his own hands that he spreads with great care as if the tires he "sees" are delicate and precious. He smiles. "Uncle John's Ford was a beautiful two-tone gray. He was meticulous."

Work hours on the Mawby farm were from seven a.m. to about five or six p.m., and Russ' uncle John didn't expect special privileges by virtue of being family. In fact, if anything, he demanded more of himself than he did of others.

"John was always at our place to work at least ten or fifteen minutes early. We had a hired man and a live-in hired girl which was fairly common pre-World War II," Russ explains. "We had another hired man who usually had lunch and dinner with us. My mother got the meals ready with the help of MaryAnn, the hired girl. We always had supper at six o'clock."

He squints, calling the images forth from the recesses of his mind as he sets the scene. His animated demeanor suggests he is enjoying reliving them.

"I can remember on one occasion specifically when the others had sat down to eat and my dad came out of the house because he noticed that John's car hadn't been moved."

His voice rises, reflecting the concern that his father felt at the time. Had something terrible happened in the orchard? Uncle John, he explained, was getting up in years but usually ended his work day with the others.

"He went out lookin' for John just as John was walking up from the orchard. He had been thinning peaches. My dad called out to him and said, 'John! You're way late!'"

"I know," John replied. "But I didn't feel I had done a fair day's work so I wasn't going to quit until I had."

Russ is contemplative for a moment. "I suppose John was making maybe three dollars a day at that time — which would have been in about 1940. I was a kid and heard this. Those are the kinds of things that stay with you forever... the kinds of values."

His voice becomes wistful as the recollections of people of the past bring a sweetness like that of the lemonade he takes a moment to enjoy.

Be a good role model. It is easy to tell just by the warmth in Russ' eyes and voice, that he respected his parents.

"My father didn't give many lectures. He taught more by example. He didn't smoke or drink and had no use for either. He didn't preach about it, would just comment once in a while. He could see that lives could be ruined by alcohol. We didn't know as much about tobacco then, but Dad was convinced that breathing in smoke and breathing out smoke, couldn't be good for a person. I have never, to this very day, ever lit a cigarette. Never. Never tried it in high school. Never went out behind the barn. Just out of respect for my dad."

His tenderness for his mother is also evident in his expressions.

"My mother was a great partner to my dad and a marvelous mother. She kept the farm books and helped sort peaches and apples, stepping in whenever and wherever needed," he recalls. "She was always available with cookies after school, as a volunteer leader in 4-H, and as a steady and loving, encouraging parent."

Trust and be trustworthy. Russ liked to ride with his father when he made calls on other fruit growers. It was often through observing his actions and listening to the farmers' conversations, that he learned more about his father's values, without those values being overtly taught.

"The men would be talking and the other farmer would say to my dad, 'Well, it's spring and they got that big dance and my boy is graduating and I haven't decided if I am going to let him take the pickup to the dance.'"

Russ smiles and winks. He knows what happens next and says with dramatic flair, "My dad would have a mortified look on his face and say, 'A pickup truck? Why, you don't want to have your son take his date to the dance in a pickup truck. Let him take the car!'"

As he alternately role plays the parts of the farmers having their springtime conversation, you can almost picture the fellows standing outside the barn or the apple storage building, leaning against an old battered pickup truck with wood-stave sides. Years of jostling across dusty rutted orchard lanes are etched into its dingy rusted frame. A good scrubbing and waxing wouldn't have helped much, and who would ever have had the time or the energy to polish a farm truck?

Even sneaking the good quilt off the back of mother's settee in the parlor to cover the wire poking through the truck's old frayed horsehair seat might not make it fit for a young lady wearing her one and only party dress.

The farmer would speak again, aghast at Mr. Mawby's suggestion that he offer his son the use of the car. "Oh, I would never trust him with the car!" he groans. "Would you?"

Mr. Mawby's answer is swift. "My gosh, who would I trust more than my own son?"

Russ feels the faith of his father across the generations and the years as if he were standing at his side even now. "That was the value system I grew up with," Russ adds with a quietness. "I knew that my father trusted me not to do anything foolish."

It is often said that we have to grow up ourselves to appreciate all the things our parents tried to teach us, and it is quite clear that Russ has spent his lifetime both appreciating and applying what he learned from his.

Build consensus. Practice fairness. "My dad taught values all the time… civic involvement… how you work through the political process to get the roads improved, how you work with township governments to deal with different problems. He always worked to build consensus and to get support for what seems to be best for the greatest number," Russ says.

You have the feeling as he speaks, that he can see his father standing up at a meeting, and having the room grow quiet because what he is about to say will have been well-considered before it is spoken.

Russ remembers too, that his parents were people of faith. Theirs was a faith shaped by difficult experiences with organized religion that led them to seek a new path which, in turn, provided another example from which the Mawby children would learn.

Share responsibility. "We were going to a particular church and the church had borrowed some money," Russ says. "My father was a member of the church board and was knowledgeable about the debt and its obligation. The note for the loan had been signed by the minister and four others. But with the Depression, everybody, including the minister, abandoned the shared responsibility. The others all turned to my father and said, 'Wes, you're the only one with any money.'"

Russ gets a dour look on his face. "Dad didn't think that was right," he says. "He was more than willing to do more than his share, but the church and its congregation had an obligation and it shouldn't all fall on one person. Dad had real trouble with organized religion after that."

The value of shared responsibility was one that Russ would call to the fore many times over his years of leadership at the Kellogg Foundation. It was not good, he maintained, for the Foundation to underwrite the entire cost of any project. There was room for seed money to get something started, or to help with a portion of some aspect of the project. But support also had to come from within the organization or the community receiving the grant money, so that responsibility, ownership, and commitment for the success of the undertaking belonged to everyone.

Similarly, Russ believed that it should not be the role of foundations to dictate to communities what their problems are, or how they should solve them. Communities themselves, he believed, were in the best position to determine their needs and should be supported as they developed the capacity to resolve problems from within.

Parents' responsibility to their children comes first. Russ and his three siblings were each born four years apart, so for sixteen years Wesley and Ruby Mawby had children in high school. But back in the 1930s, children didn't wait at the end of their driveway to board a big yellow bus that hustled them off to school. Those were the days before school consolidation and bussing. So, morning and night, either parent saw to it that the children were taken the seven miles to school and picked up at the end of the day.

"They encouraged us to participate in things like the junior class play, band or other activities," Russ says, keenly aware of just how important the sacrifice was to his early education. "It was an amazing commitment without any fanfare. That's just the way it was. They believed that it was right that we go to school and that we had the other opportunities as well, even if they were inconvenienced." Together the Mawbys had made the decision to be parents, and together they shared the responsibility. Neither saw parenting as something to be relegated to whatever hours were left after a career or a personal pursuit.

Russ Mawby grew up in an age when few ever questioned the right of a parent to mete out punishment with a willow switch to the backside. Such discipline was not necessary in the Mawby household.

"A stern look did wonders," Russ says with a wry grin. "I don't remember ever being spanked, although I was dressed down on two or three occasions. Overall, I was a pretty good kid and wanted to please my parents. I was quick to finish my homework, my 4-H and Scouting projects, and even to practice the cornet. I don't ever remember being grounded per se."

It has been many years since Russ has put a cornet to his lips and summoned forth a tune, but the look on his face suggests that he probably would still try it if his parents were there to listen. And they, being good parents, would tell him how wonderful his music sounded.

Select the right mate. Russ' face grows wistful when he speaks of his late wife Ruth, and the fifty years they shared. But a confession slips out and with it an impish grin. He admits, that before he noticed the young Ruth Edison, he noticed her father's team of Percheron work horses.

In the mid-part of the twentieth century, when an especially well-matched work or driving team was envied as much as a sleek sports car or powerful SUV would be today, Art Edison had one of the finest work teams in the area. The young Russ Mawby had been to the Edison farm with his father on several occasions, and was in awe of the team.

"I had known Ruth only as Art Edison's daughter," Russ says. "It was that team of Percherons Art had, that I really loved!" He laughs a deep hearty laugh, swirls the ice in his lemonade, and is a young man again.

"It was the summer of '49. I had graduated that June and had a job as an assistant 4-H club agent in Kent County. Ruth, who was a few years older than I, was the home demonstration agent. We were leaders to the young people at 4-H camp. She had responsibility for the girls. I was in charge of the boys, so we worked together. It was there that I saw her basic values – like being willing to get up at two a.m. with a little girl who was homesick or had a stomach ache."

The values of the Edison family and the Mawby family were very similar. The Edison family also was well established – about four generations had grown up on their fruit farm.

"They believed in education as we did," Russ explains, "although they were more likely to have gone to a symphony than we. We would never have gone to a symphony!"

His face lights up in a big smile, seeing in his mind's eye, a team of Percherons, a young woman caring for a homesick youngster, and perhaps the curious image of himself at the symphony.

"Ruth was a great lady," he says reverently.

Of their early courtship, Ruth is said to have told a reporter, "I don't know if I swept him off his feet, but I do know that he chased me until I let him catch me." Ruth was unpretentious and always gracious.

Ruth Edison was a pioneer of sorts, launching a career, albeit traditionally female, at a time when many women sought neither a college degree nor a career. She used her degree in home economics from Western Michigan University to teach at Wyoming High School near Grand Rapids before becoming a home demonstration agent in Kent County, the point at which she and Russ became better acquainted. She even had her own regular radio program in which she offered tips on home extension topics.

After Russ and Ruth were married in mid-December 1950, Russ used an Army deferral to complete his master's degree in agricultural economics at Purdue University in Indiana. When he wasn't called up for the service, he began working on a doctoral degree back at MSU and took a position as an extension specialist in marketing in the department of agricultural economics. He had only his final exams and dissertation to complete when, in October 1953, the Army called.

The young couple packed up a few belongings and spent much of the next two years living in a two-room apartment at Fort Smith, Arkansas, where he was assigned to the field artillery. He rose to what he calls the "lofty rank of corporal" and could have gone on to officers' school had he chosen to remain in the military. But, he is quick to point out, "I would rather develop young people than be in the business of killing them."

The military, even apart from war-time operations, was not what he envisioned for a career, so when he mustered out he returned to MSU to wrap up the doctoral program in agricultural economics in 1959.

Ruth, meanwhile, left her career to give her full support to Russ and to the nurturing of the three children they adopted, siblings Doug and David, who had been through a series of foster home placements, and a girl, Karen.

Even as she took on the responsibility of parenting, Ruth continued the family tradition of being active in volunteer roles with 4-H, the church, and various civic organizations.

Throughout their years together, Ruth was the consummate support-

Russ and Ruth

ive helpmate, confidant, and partner. Like her executive husband, she could dine graciously with heads of state, but be equally content serving coffee at their country church. She had the insightfulness to offer wise counsel throughout his many leadership roles but never sought to upstage him. Her greatest happiness came from doing whatever was needed to make their relationship and family strong and secure.

When she left earthly service she was at home with Russ at her side.

Be the best at whatever you are called to be. (Even if you didn't apply for the job.) Russ is not joking when he says he has never applied for a job in his life. Of course, it can be assumed that he must have been doing something fairly well to have been tapped for the positions he has held.

Back at MSU that "tap" came again.

"My life was going along just fine," he recalls. Military service was behind him and he had eagerly resumed extension work.

"Then one day I got a call that the dean wanted to see me," he says, leaning forward, wringing his hands.

"I thought to myself, Oh no, what's wrong now?" He feigns a worried look, but not very convincingly.

"There was the dean, Thomas K. Cowden, with the director of extension, Paul Miller, and they said they wanted me to become the assistant director of extension. They hadn't talked with me about it at all! They had talked with MSU's president, John Hannah, and they had all agreed that that was the right thing to do. So, at twenty-eight, they had the audacity to name me the assistant director of cooperative extension!"

Russ is reflective and deliberate for a few moments, explaining that it was at that time as he moved from agent to administrator that he began to think a career in administration might be possible. He envisioned himself moving through the ranks within cooperative extension to become a director, then a dean, and maybe one day even the president of MSU or another major university. Ambitious plans for a young man just named to his first administrative role.

Life became more complicated as an administrator, but once again Russ and his young family settled into a new routine that soon led to full professorship and the directorship of cooperative extension programs. The plan was beginning to unfold.

Then, in 1964, there was that "tap" again. Would he be interested in meeting with Emory Morris and Phillip Blackerby, president and vice president of the W. K. Kellogg Foundation in Battle Creek, to discuss joining the Foundation's staff?

Most young professionals would have jumped at the chance and still would today.

Not so Russ Mawby.

"I was happy doing what I was doing at MSU," he said.

It took some cajoling, but Russ accepted the invitation to at least learn about the position.

With Ruth, his number one business partner, he drove to Battle Creek, had lunch accompanied by an offer he couldn't refuse, and became director of the Foundation's division of agriculture.

The dream of one day advancing to the top of an organization unfolded when, six years later, he became the Foundation's CEO. Not surprisingly, more than once over those years he was courted to leave the Foundation and become a university president, the very position to which he thought he had aspired. Each time he politely declined.

"My peers respected me, but I had come to feel that if I was going to leave foundation work I would rather be head of a small, Christian, liberal arts college where I felt I could be close to the faculty, students, alumni, and the community," he explains, his tone clearly conveying that he has never doubted his decision. "I could teach a class, have a coke in the student union with the young people, and make a real difference. I wanted to be close to people who make things work, because, in the final analysis, only people matter. Only people are important."

He becomes very studious and serious, perhaps retracing the footsteps of his career.

"You have to have people who believe in the organization and in making things work no matter how you redraw the lines," he says, slipping easily back into the voice of a leader who knows how to get things done. "The board of directors has to be behind it. It is the same whether in the nonprofit or for-profit sectors."

Do things right and do the right things. I asked Russ how a leader remains true to values of integrity and honesty amid all the pressures and politics of the business and philanthropic worlds.

Russ shakes his head ruefully. "If you really believe in what is right, there should not be an inconsistency between values and success. The standards now in some of the corporate world are really disgusting, but these people doing the things we are reading about, know that what they are doing is wrong.

"I am an unsophisticated person. A shirtsleeve executive is what I've been called, and I take it as a compliment. I have certain values that I believe are right and I live those consistently. There is no discontinuity between who I am and what I do."

He doesn't say any of this with arrogance but with resolve, certain beyond any doubt of its correctness.

Select your friends carefully. Until this point in our visit, Russ has been modest, self-effacing, and reflective, resting casually against the cushions of the sofa. But suddenly his voice changes as an air of great self-importance comes over him. He straightens his back and lifts his chin.

"Did you know that I have never given a poor speech?" he says, patting his chest. He studies my face to gauge my reaction. I know him well enough to tell when he is bluffing.

"It's true you know," he adds, still trying (without success) to appear pompous. But he cannot maintain the pretense, and quickly reveals a lesson he has learned over his years as a high-profile, powerful executive whom everyone seeks to please.

"Only your closest friends are willing to tell you if you've not done something well, and in some cases with some leaders, even their friends won't last until tomorrow if they are honest," he adds.

He offers sage advice. "You select your friends carefully and you nurture those relationships."

Have a place of peaceful refuge. Everyone needs a place of refuge and release from the stresses of life. Some pick up a golf club, others a fishing rod. Until neuropathy left him unable to walk without extreme difficulty, for Russ the place of refuge was with his horses or in his flower garden. Except for the times when he was traveling, which were substantial during his Foundation years, he did his own barn chores before and after work.

"It was the quiet of the barn, the nearness of the horses that gave solid continuity to my day," he says.

His voice is calm, yet because of his current physical difficulties, it is tinged with longing too. "If the day had been frustrating I could come home and work it through as I did farm chores. I could keep things in balance and in perspective that way. I was never one to stop on the way home and have three drinks, followed by another one when I got home. That was never a part of my life. Never.

"The setting of Mother Nature and God's good earth have been precious to me in giving me continuity. I could mend a board in the fence or talk to the horses. Each of my animals has a personality. Each is an individual. They have a social order that they arrange and administer very effectively. Being with them is my version of 'Happy Hour.'"

Believe in divine intervention. After his retirement from the daily demands of his career, and then just five years later, the loss of his dearest companion, Russ found himself at loose ends. He was still very involved in his community, church, and favorite causes, but life had lost its luster.

Strangely, the same thing was happening at the same time for another person, Lou Ann Sherman. Lou Ann had been Russ' first secretary when he joined the Kellogg Foundation staff. Over the years each held the other in great respect. They knew one another's spouses and children. They delighted as their respective families grew and careers flourished.

Lou Ann became Russ' administrative assistant in his last years with the Foundation and was a helpmate to him and Ruth as Ruth's health declined. The women admired one another and shared many of the same qualities.

When Lou Ann retired from the Foundation and her husband, Jim, from his career, they had retirement plans ready to realize – traveling, spending time with their grandchildren, and savoring the benefits of their years of work.

But tragically, that was not to be. Jim died as the result of injuries suffered in a fall from the roof of their home as he was making repairs. By the summer of 2000, both Russ and Lou Ann found themselves without their dearest companions. Each was adrift.

Russ was not accustomed to attending community events without Ruth at his side, and knowing that Lou Ann was as alone as he, invited her to accompany him on one such outing. After knowing one another as colleagues for more than thirty years, they saw one another in an entirely new way.

A year after Ruth's death, they were married in a private family ceremony. The respect and friendship they share, is a wonderful extension of that which they knew as colleagues.

"I know that it is divine intervention that has guided my life," Russ says. "There have been so many wonderful people who have been a part of my life. I had a wonderful person for a wife to share my life with for fifty years and then, to be blessed with a second wonderful person to share the remaining years with is a gift. I have told Lou Ann that she is my angel and she is, she is indeed."

Russ, of course, had no idea when he proposed marriage that neuropathy would so quickly rob him of full mobility, a reality that both frustrates and saddens him. He had great plans for the places in the world he wanted Lou Ann to see and the things they could enjoy together at their home where a foal frolics by its mother in a pasture near the house and the inimitable Sí Señor, as senior states-man, still keeps watch over his domain (just don't ask him his age).

Lou Ann and Russ

Lou Ann, who perhaps never expected to find herself sharing a love for horses, much less talking to them, has settled happily into a new lifestyle. In her ever gracious manner she softly repeats her wedding vows and with a smile says, "Russ and I take care of one another."

Lou Ann is modest about considering herself to be Russ' angel and he is equally modest about the dozens of honors he has received over the years, including being named by The *Detroit News* in 1994 as one of only 12 Michiganians to be featured as "Angels Among Us" for their selfless works to benefit others.

He is unpretentious in part, because he knows his position at the head of a philanthropic organization made him an obvious target to be wooed in the hopes of securing a grant or a good word. And, he knows that sometimes the lines get blurred in the public's mind between a founda-tion executive's personal and professional philanthropy. Russ is clear in his own mind about the differences, and about what motivates him to be personally generous, apart from the role he carried out on behalf of the Kellogg Foundation.

While some might question the wisdom of a man who only owns the back half of race horses or takes the advice of a miniature donkey, Russ has done well for himself over the years, but chooses to follow the biblical edict not to store up earthly treasures.

Instead, he has carefully and conscientiously chosen not to "spend" money but to "invest" it in people.

"Ruth and I always felt blessed that we had more material goods than we ever anticipated," Russ says with humility. "People were surprised that we didn't move to a bigger house or to the lake. That's not to be critical of the people who have, but that was not what we wanted. We provided for our children, we traveled, and I insisted that the Foundation not treat me any differently than it did program staff. I want to share my good fortune because I know what a difference opportunities provided for me by others – even strangers I've never met – have made in my life."

Some of the gifts made by the Mawbys bear their name, others have been made in complete and insistent anonymity. But the gifts have been as much in time and talent as they have in dollars. Russ has served on boards of a long list of corporations and nonprofits including the Michigan 4-H Foundation and Youth for Understanding. He has been an advisor to governors and to the board of elders of his church where, in his rich deep voice, he sometimes reads the Bible lesson.

Through it all, remembering the lessons taught by his parents, Russ Mawby has been mindful of the importance of people working together and sharing responsibility, for the successful accomplishment of an under-taking.

"Only people are important. Only people make the difference," he will say again, using one of the familiar Mawbyisms for which he is so famous.

It is true that only people make the difference, but it deserves to be said that some people make a much greater difference. Russ Mawby is one such person.

Kaylowa

"Don't even try to see her. She's been sold again so there's no point in it."
There was unmistakable finality in the dealer's voice.
Ruth could see on Russ' face that this time he knew it was over.
Something bad had happened to Kaylowa. He was sure of it.

This was not your average auction of average horses in a dusty ring at a dingy livestock exchange.

Not a chance.

This was the prestigious annual "Super Sale" in Scottsdale, Arizona, where pricey cocktails and a big name performer opened the "show" and where red-tinted, glitter-dusted sawdust sparkled against a royal blue backdrop in the sales arena.

No well-worn riding boots or faded blue jeans here. Attendees to this event wore business suits and shimmering cocktail dresses, confirming the one hundred thousand-dollar line of credit that got them through the door.

No rough plank bleacher seats here, either. When the announcer called out "Let the sale begin!" prospective bidders and anxious sellers made their way to red velvet theatre seats.

While ringmasters in white tails presented each horse in turn, buyers signaled their bids, and sellers tracked the numbers in slick sales catalogs.

Understandably, there were no pigeon-toed ponies or sway-backed saddle horses in this, the 1984 sales lot. Only thirty-seven horses would enter the arena and these were the finalists from some six hundred-fifty inspected by a team of experts who had combed the country to determine which exquisite equines possessed the right stuff for the sale. There had been bloodline studies and vet checks, performance reviews and certifications. The owners of the finalists had each paid several thousand dollars just for the privilege of having his or her animal in the sale.

Horse lovers and owners, Russ and Ruth Mawby of Augusta, Michigan, were among the people in formal attire making small talk before the sale, though they found themselves anxiously wondering, *Did we do the right thing to come here?*

What the Mawbys had done was offer up for sale the treasure of their stable, at first not thinking that their fine eight-year-old, copper-colored Arabian mare might make the final cut. But this horse, like the sale she was about to be part of, was no ordinary horse.

As with so many other things in American culture that change in popularity from year to year – car styles, clothing, and cuisine – what fetches high prices in the horse industry also changes from year to year. In 1984, offspring of the famous Arabian stallion, *Bask, imported to the U.S. from Poland, had suddenly begun commanding phenomenal prices – six figures and above. (*Appears before the name to denote that the horse has been imported to the United States.) The Mawbys just happened to have one such *Bask offspring in their ordinary barn on their ordinary farm in Augusta. That horse was Russ' beloved bay mare named Baskaylowa.

Baskaylowa had been a part of the Mawby family since her birth on the farm in June of 1976. She was the daughter of Alowa, a descendant of one of the original Arabian horses imported to the U.S. from England many years earlier by W.K. Kellogg of Kellogg cereal fame, and the creator of the foundation which bears his name.

Russ Mawby was well acquainted with the Kellogg herd maintained at California State Polytechnic at Pomona. Successor to W.K. Kellogg and Emory Morris as chief executive officer of the Kellogg Foundation, Russ had bought Alowa as a nine-year old in 1973, directly from the Kellogg herd and two years later had her bred to *Bask. Beautiful Baskaylowa with the star on her forehead, white front fetlocks, and dark mane and tail was the child of that courtship.

A horse lover since he was a farm boy in the 1930s, Russ was with Alowa when she foaled at his Rimy Mead Farm (Rimy Mead is an English term meaning "frosty meadows"). He spent much of that night on an old cot in the barn waiting for the foal to be born. Near daybreak, Baskaylowa entered the world and Russ was there, bleary-eyed but attentive. A pink flag, indicating the new arrival was a filly, was quickly and happily run up the "foal pole" near the barn.

"We'll name her Baskaylowa," Russ told Ruth as they admired their new arrival.

"Kaylowa for short," she suggested with a grin.

Eye-catching and crowd-pleasing Kaylowa, earned top honors in equitation and conformation at regional shows throughout the Midwest. She handled herself with such carriage and grace that she had earned seventy of the seventy-five points required to hold "Legion of Merit" status in the Arabian Horse Association. Darn near perfect.

But Kaylowa had achieved absolute perfection by nuzzling her way right into Russ' heart every time he went out to the barn to do chores before and after going to work at the Kellogg Foundation's offices in Battle Creek.

Unaware of her own importance or perhaps kept humble by her barn mates, Kaylowa shared quarters with a pair of Polled Hereford oxen, named Yankee and Doodle, who held the unparalleled honor of having paraded down Constitution Avenue in Washington, D.C., for the nation's Bicentennial, and a miniature donkey named Sí Señor, self-appointed supervisor of the Rimy Mead barn and pastures.

"Kaylowa, I don't know why you have to be so special to me," Russ would tell her as if the elegant mare understood every word. "But you are special and you know it."

He taught Kaylowa to shake "hands," something she did not consider herself too important to do, knowing that the handshake was always rewarded with a generous measure of affection and a sugar cube or two.

Having horses was more about giving love than about making money, and to have a horse out of the Kellogg herd, for Russ, was more about sentiment and fondness for the Kellogg name than about investment opportunities.

Still, Russ understood business, including the unpredictability of stock markets and horse markets, both of which can be risky. And he knew when Baskaylowa's father, the great stallion *Bask died, that her value would instantly increase. What he hadn't counted on was that as her potential worth steadily rose, he would begin to agonize over the practicalities of business versus pleasure, no matter how much he loved the mare.

"Ruth, I know it doesn't make sense to keep Kaylowa," he reasoned uneasily more than once, as associates who knew the Kellogg Arabian horse bloodlines and the changing marketplace, kept him informed of her ever-rising value.

"But how can you part with her?" Ruth asked, trying to make certain he had given the whole matter thorough consideration. "You know how you feel about that horse."

"It's the realities of the market," he replied as matter-of-factly as possible. "The market for *Bask horses is getting to be unreal, just unreal."

"Unreal? What do you mean?"

"I mean that *Bask horses are selling in the hundreds of thousands of dollars now. With my interest being what it is — enjoyment more than anything — it makes economic sense to sell Kaylowa and get a less valuable horse to have around here. I don't feel right having one mare worth that much money in my barn."

"If it's what you want," Ruth said, a look of uncertainty crossing her face. If this was what her husband thought was the right thing to do, then she would support him in it. But it didn't feel like the right thing to her, knowing how fond he was of the mare.

"I think it's for the best," he concluded. "I will submit her for consideration for the Scottsdale sale."

Baskaylowa, in foal to another fine Arabian stallion, passed the intense scrutiny of the panel of judges selecting the finalists for the Scottsdale sale, an accomplishment that Russ was not sure made him feel as good as it should have. Kaylowa was quickly transported to a Kentucky horse farm where she foaled, was bred back immediately to *Aladdin, the successor to *Bask, and then taken by trailer to Arizona. There, she would be readied for the big sale that would draw buyers and sellers from across the United States and several foreign countries.

"Are you sure this is what you want to do?" Ruth plied gently as the days to the big sale of 1984 ticked away. She could see that Russ was as anxious about the whole situation as he had been when he awaited Kaylowa's birth.

"I made the decision and I can't second-guess myself," he answered. "It's done."

Then, too soon, it was sale day.

Amid the glitter and glimmer, Sammy Davis Jr. opened the event with a rousing performance. By the time the first horse was led into the theatre the audience was primed, the adrenaline flowing.

"Kaylowa will be number nineteen," Russ said, scanning the program, suddenly wishing he could swap his black tuxedo for blue jeans and the fanfare for his farm. He lowered his voice and whispered to Ruth, "I think she could bring as much as a hundred thousand. That will cover what we have into her in breeding, training, and care, plus give us even a little extra. That's good enough."

Ruth studied his face and reached for his hand. She knew him better than anyone. His voice could have been more convincing. How can "good enough" make up for "good bye"?

It soon looked as if Russ' hopes for how much Kaylowa might bring could be realized. Lot number one was a trio of mares that, together, landed more than three and a half million dollars. The second horse offered was the world's reigning reserve champion Arabian mare. Bidding did not stop until it had topped two and half million.

Russ Mawby was on the edge of his seat. With each successive *Bask descendant brought into the auction ring to walk, trot, and strut its stuff, he grew more anxious. With each bang of the auctioneer's gavel he wrote the final bid beside each horse's name. Some brought as little as fifty thousand dollars and others continued to top six figures.

"And next into the arena, ladies and gentlemen, is the elegant mare, Baskaylowa!" boomed the auctioneer's voice with great flair.

"This is it," Ruth said, almost prayerfully. "This is it."

Kaylowa was led into the theatre to a chorus of appreciative "Ohhhhs." Her copper coat glowed against the glittering sawdust and the backdrop of the blue-draped stage, accented by pots of red and white geraniums.

The bidding began at twenty-five thousand dollars. "Do I hear…?" called the auctioneer. Hands went up.

"Do I hear….?" Still more hands. Again and again.

Russ and Ruth Mawby watched in astonishment. Finally, the gavel was sounded. Baskaylowa had brought far more than her owners had hoped she might. But their elation was subdued by sadness. When the sale was over they would be returning to Michigan without her. She was no longer theirs, the favorite child of Rimy Mead farm.

The place that Kaylowa held in Russ Mawby's heart was still hers and hers alone. When he went to the barn to do chores, there was no special nicker of greeting, no Kaylowa to willingly raise her right front leg to shake "hands," no muzzle pressed to his pocket to find the sugar cubes or carrots hidden there, and no magnificent thunder of hooves across the pasture as only Kaylowa could run, with her head aloft and her tail arched in that distinctive Arabian flair. He sought not to second guess his decision. But he missed his copper-coated friend.

For the next eleven years, Russ and Ruth continued to follow Kaylowa's life. It was not, they learned with sadness, one of happily-ever-afters as a contended brood mare, grazing in green pastures with a playful foal at her side. Their beloved mare was sold again and again, leaving Arizona to go to New York, and New York to Florida, and Florida to Alabama, and then back to Florida again.

As the Mawbys followed her moves they tried repeatedly to buy Kaylowa back.

"This is Russ Mawby calling from Michigan…," his calls began as he outlined his hopes for each successive owner. Sometimes he and Ruth visited Kaylowa who remembered them as much as they remembered her. But each time they tried, no deal could be reached, and they sadly returned home with an empty trailer.

"Do you think we should have offered more money?" Ruth asked after each unsuccessful attempt.

"No," Russ would reply. "We have to work within current market terms and we've done that and more. Every time we have gone through this, her value has become less because she is getting older. We've been more than fair." Still, discouragement permeated his words and thoughts.

It wasn't as if the Rimy Mead barn was empty. There were other horses to occupy Russ' attention. He had harness race horses that he often told people were the most polite horses anyone might own, the kind of horse that would tell its competitors at the track, "Oh you go ahead. I wouldn't think of crossing the finish line first."

There were Haflingers, an Austrian breed of miniature draft horse that resembles Belgians, and are striking in appearance with broad muscular shoulders, well-rounded hind quarters, and thick white or cream manes and tails to complement chestnut coats. These, he affectionately called "Ruth's horses." The Mawbys delighted in hitching them to an old sleigh that Ruth's grandfather had purchased many years earlier from the Grand Rapids Fire Department at the time it switched from genuine horsepower to the more modern variety.

Then, of course, there was still the inimitable Sí Señor, who compensated for his lack of stature or elegance, with sincerity and ears.

In March of 1995, as Russ and Ruth prepared to leave Michigan for their annual winter retreat to the warmer climes of Florida, Kaylowa's name came up again. Russ was keenly aware that the mare, now approaching twenty years of age, was still in Florida.

"We've got to try to get her back again," Russ said to Ruth as they tucked the last of their things in suitcases for the trip. "One more time."

"The last time you tried," Ruth reminded him, "you offered well above her value. You've said yourself that her potential as a good brood mare is pretty much gone, yet they still refused your offer."

"I know."

"Well then?"

"One last time. I would like to try just one last time," he said, noting the look of doubt that swept across her face. Normally she was supportive of just about anything he suggested, but this time her face told a different story.

"I suppose we could try," she began hesitantly, shrugging her shoulders and sighing loudly. "But I don't think it will do any good." She was trying to let him down gently and prepare him for another disappointment.

One might think that after eleven years a horse wouldn't still have that much hold on a person. Time heals all wounds, as the saying goes, but it is equally said that absence makes the heart grow fonder.

Russ contacted a horse buyer in Florida and asked him to see about Kaylowa and try to negotiate a deal for her. The two men talked at length, weighing considerations to be made, depending on what condition the mare might be in, and other factors that would affect her value one way or another.

"I want Kaylowa," Russ insisted. "I am willing to go above her actual value just to be able to bring her home. You are authorized to offer...."

A short time later, the anticipated return phone call came.

"What did you find out?" Russ asked eagerly, all set to add, "When can we arrange to pick her up?"

There was a long silence at the other end of the line. Finally, the buyer spoke, his voice cool. "Couldn't get her."

"Couldn't get Kaylowa?" Russ was shocked. "Is she all right? How did she look? Why wouldn't they sell?"

The horse buyer was evasive.

Russ was disheartened. Something in the buyer's voice suggested to him that something might be wrong with Kaylowa. He tried to press further, asking still more questions. Maybe he should go visit the owner himself?

"Don't even try to see her. She's been sold again so there's no point in it." There was unmistakable finality in the dealer's voice.

Ruth could see on Russ' face that this time he knew it was over. Something bad had happened to Kaylowa. He was sure of it.

Ruth studied his face. Normally a person who could find the good in every situation, this time Russ could think of nothing positive to say.

Ruth turned away. She couldn't bear to tell her soulmate of more than forty years that she had played a role in his being told not to see Kaylowa. It would have broken his heart. Ruth had told the buyer to discourage Russ. She had withheld the truth.

This, Russ decided, was the last time he would attempt to get the Arabian mare back.

"I won't say anything more about Kaylowa," Russ promised his wife. "There just doesn't seem to be anything more I can do. It's over."

Not a man to live in the past or second-guess the decisions he made in business or in his personal life, Russ did not dwell on the loss of the mare. There was plenty else to occupy his thoughts. After thirty-one years with the Kellogg Foundation, he was preparing to retire. There were many major decisions to be made, not the least of which was working with the Board to name his successor, and making the transition in leadership as smooth as possible. There were decisions to be made about which of his many other prestigious board affiliations and leadership roles to relinquish so that he could be at home more to be of help to Ruth as she began dialysis for her diabetes, and endured the discouragement that accompanies the loss of strength to post-polio syndrome and arthritis.

Meanwhile, Baskaylowa moved away and Russ moved on.

Anyone who knew the Mawbys knew that they loved their country lifestyle. Organizers for a city-wide event in honor of his years of service to the Foundation and the community, created a gala "Day on the Farm" at the city's downtown Kellogg Arena. The arena had hosted big-name entertainers, even monster trucks and the famous Lippizan stallions, but never a collection of farm animals, and more than a thousand people dressed in blue jeans or bib overalls, accented by custom-made MSU Spartan-green bandanas. There were no cocktails or fancy hors d'oeuvres, just meat loaf and chicken, apple and cherry pie. No stretch limousine for the guests of honor, just a farm cart pulled by an ox, that delivered Russ and Ruth right to center stage.

A video was shown highlighting Russ' impressive career in philanthropy and his personal involvements with the community, his family, and even his horses. As images of Baskaylowa flashed across the screen, he wondered for a fleeting moment whether he might try, when all the retirement festivities and formalities were over, just one more time to find her.

Toward the end of the evening, celebration organizers gathered to present the Mawbys with a gift to thank them for their many years of service to the community.

A collective "Ohhhh" reminiscent of that which had gone up many years earlier at a horse auction in Arizona, swept the room as a beautiful copper-coated mare with a white star on her forehead and white on her front fetlocks was led into the room.

Kaylowa!

Ruth, with tears in her eyes, sneaked a peek at her husband as he gasped in disbelief.

Tears filled Russ' eyes as he stepped from the platform and went to greet his long-lost friend. The crowd was on its feet. After eleven years apart, as he bent forward and whispered, "Kaylowa, let's shake hands," up came the mare's right front hoof to meet his outstretched hand.

An entire community that had contributed to the Kaylowa fund, had guarded the secret all those weeks! There was barely a dry eye in the house.

It had been three months since Ruth and the horse buyer co-conspired to get Baskaylowa back, once and for all. When the mare was located in the South, she was out of condition after having just foaled. She was nothing more than another horse in a barn among much younger stock. Her owners had no particular interest in keeping her.

Kaylowa was secretly returned to Michigan where she was nursed and loved back to glowing health by the equine veterinary students at Michigan State University, Russ' beloved alma mater. Over those several weeks of adoring attention, she regained the sheen in her coat, the light in her eye, and the spring in her step.

Russ Mawby and Kaylowa reunited
Photo courtesy of Russ Mawby

That evening after the celebration, Kaylowa was taken home to Rimy Mead. She backed easily out of the horse trailer and walked as contentedly into the barn and to her old feedbox as if she had only been away a short while.

"Are you coming in?" Ruth said, as the truck and trailer left the farm and the couple stood side by side under the glow of the yardlight.

"I think I might just go out to the barn for a while," Russ said, kissing his wife and thanking her again as he had several times already, for her role in bringing Kaylowa home. "I just need to spend a little time talking to Kaylowa," His eyes had a sparkle brighter than any glitter in the sawdust at that Scottsdale sale of long ago.

Ruth watched as her husband strode across the driveway to the barn, his tall figure illuminated by the light on the same pole where once Kaylowa's arrival had been proudly announced by a pink flag many years earlier.

"I'll leave a light on for you," she said.

It would be a long while before Russ would return to the house that night. He and Kaylowa had a lot of catching up to do.

Two years later, despite her advancing age, the Mawbys had Kaylowa bred one last time. She gave birth to First Star, sired by MSU Vital Signs, a great grandson of the famed *Bask. Russ and Ruth celebrated the birth by hosting an "open barn" party at their farm. Dress for the occasion, they wrote on the invitation, was to be "denim or casual, although the guests of honor will be in tails."

Kaylowa's lovely daughter could do well in competition, given her looks and lineage, but that is not in the plans. She's learned some manners, including how to shake hands like her famous mother, but she'll not go on the show circuit or to the auction ring.

"Mom and daughter are enjoying the good life and will stay right here at home," says Russ. "I have given them my word. We shook hands on it."

An Ordinary Fish

*In spite of having swallowed warm water to keep my throat clear and moist, my
vocal chords were suddenly and undeniably clogged with pond sediment.*

Memories of the joy I'd found expressing my faith in song in high
school and college, embraced me like a dear friend when I began attending services at a lovely country church.   The small but spirited choir was
much like the one I'd been part of back in Stephenson, Michigan, thirty
years earlier. There, in a town with a population of fewer than a thousand
and our church membership far fewer than that, I had the opportunity to
be a "big fish in a little pond," as the saying goes. When there was a
special solo to be sung, it was usually given to mature, mellow-throated
Leota, or teenage, tentative me.   The congregation was appreciative no
matter which of us sang.

Now, after all these years, wistful recollections tugged at me. Should
I join the choir? Or, might it be better to confine my crooning to an audience limited to soap in the shower, weeds in the garden, or my horse under
saddle?

When I left home in the fall of 1971 to attend Albion College, a small,
liberal arts college in southern Michigan, I wanted just about as much as
I have ever wanted anything, to sing in its highly-acclaimed, hundred-plus
voice choir. Beth Brown, church choir director back home, was an Albion
grad and had influenced my decision to attend her beloved alma mater.

"I just know you can make it into the choir!" Beth said. "You must
audition!"

The college choir director, David Strickler, affectionately known as

"Mr. Dave," had a reputation for being exceptionally demanding. Those who survived auditions with him were the cream of the crop.

Could I? Should I? I had sung solos back home, after all.

One by one, dozens of choir hopefuls trooped into the college's Goodrich Chapel that late summer at the start of my freshman year. With sweaty palms and a racing heart, I waited with my peers in the long hallway outside the double-doors to the choir room. Each of us in turn would be handed a sheet of music and after having only moments to scan it, would be asked to sing a page or two. Mr. Dave and the student president of the choir, would scrutinize each wanna-be's pitch, posture, poise, and presentation.

Many hopefuls joked casually or warmed up with soft "la-la-la's" and "do-re-me's." Few showed so much as a hint of anxiety, and as each took his or her turn, I understood why. These were exquisite voices, undeniably a blend of God-given talent and professional training. Many were also polished performers, having sung in metropolitan churches and even professional theatres while yet in high school. Their voices were awesome.

Then there was me – the big fish in the little pond which seemed to be evaporating into a puddle as the line ahead of me grew shorter. I was rapidly becoming a fish out of water, flapping desperately about.

I tried some positive self-talk. *You've had piano lessons, you can read music, you have perfect pitch, you... you... are scared to death*!

I struggled through the audition.

When the list of names of new members was later posted on the choir room doors, as I feared, mine was not among them.

"Don't give up," one of the successfuls soothed, seeing disappointment emblazoned on my face like a scarlet letter. "You're taking voice lessons this semester, right? Maybe you can try again next semester."

"Yah, maybe," I told her with about as much hope as a one-finned tuna in a school of sharks. "Maybe."

From the first voice lesson under the tutelage of Albion College's Jackie Maag, I knew, that she knew, I would never be transformed into performance material unless it was through divine intervention. (Jesus performed miracles with fish, but not the kind I desperately needed.) I also knew that Miss Maag would do her best to help me reach the limits of my potential. The sad truth was that it probably wouldn't take her very long to get there.

"You've got to bring the sound up from deep under the diaphragm, Janice," she would say, demonstrating by arching her back, pushing the tips of her fingers under her rib cage, taking in a large full breath, and then breaking forth in a rich mezzo soprano voice. "Like this, Janice. Like this."

She started me out on lovely old ballads and by the end of the semester, when voice students had to perform individually before a panel of music department faculty, I did my best not to cause the composer of a wonderful Latin aria to turn over in his grave.

As I anxiously scanned the faces of the faculty, it was difficult to decipher the meaning of the smiles. Had I come that far in one semester of voice lessons or were they merely humored by my naïve courage?

It was Miss Maag who pleaded my case to Mr. Dave. "Janice would benefit greatly from being in the choir," she said, knowing full well his exacting standards. "I'd like very much for you to give her a chance."

Mr. Dave wanted his choir to maintain its impeccable reputation yet he also wanted students to fulfill their dreams. I suspect that my saving grace was that while my voice was not particularly forceful, I could read music, and could carry a tune without the need for a ten-gallon pail. If I could not do the choir any good, perhaps I would do it no harm, suggesting perhaps that a Hippocratic Oath for vocalists might not be such a bad idea.

Mr. Dave relented, and this fish suddenly became a guppy in an ocean rich with exotic species. I was the happiest guppy alive. I thrilled at how the distinctly different sections of sopranos and altos melded with the tenors, baritones and basses to create a whole and harmoniously spirited sound that could hold an audience in its spell. I loved touring to other cities and states to perform in stunningly beautiful churches, and to watch every fiber in Mr. Dave's wiry little frame analyze the acoustical nuances of each sanctuary, and the distinctive character of its organ as we gathered for rehearsal. He absorbed the sense of the place and then summoned forth from us every subtlety in our voices that would make everything work together for greatest effect.

I also knew beyond a doubt, that singing was a way to express my faith, not only in moments of happiness, but also in times of discouragement. The rigors of the academic environment and the realities of simply being on the threshold of adulthood, delivered challenges unlike any before, and distinctly different from any since. That phase of my life offered its own music, however strained the melody seemed at times.

Now, all these years later, while listening to the choir at this lovely little church, memories from long ago crowded into mind. The urge to sing was irrepressible as I watched this group celebrate faith.

Somewhat hesitantly, I slipped into the pew with the sopranos at a Wednesday night rehearsal. The choir and Patti, its witty, good-humored director, welcomed me with delight and, gratefully, no audition. Whatever Jackie Maag might have accomplished with my voice in 1971 was long-gone. Fortunately, everyone was just like me – singing for pure joy. We were all ordinary fish in an ordinary pond.

I was very surprised when at rehearsal one evening, Patti asked, "Jan, do you want to try the solo?"

We were soon going to be singing a lovely anthem, "Come Follow Me," that began with a short, simple soprano solo.

It had been so-o-o long....

"Sure," I said, feeling strangely like a gasping guppy the moment the word crossed my lips.

The opening solo was only seventeen measures. Surely I could manage that.

But after the first couple runs-through, I was convinced that this fish had leaped too soon, not paying nearly enough attention to the size of the hook that had lodged itself sharply in my throat.

Choir members were gracious as I squeaked and squawked. Then Patti asked one of the men to set up a microphone.

"Oh no!" I protested. "All anybody in the congregation will hear is the sound of my heart thumping like crazy!"

She would not be swayed. "Your voice is so soft that without the microphone, some of the congregation, especially those with hearing problems won't hear you at all."

Hearing problems? I thought. That's a relief!

As the days ticked away, I wanted to call Patti and offer a marvelous alternative. The choir, I reasoned, could hum the melody softly in the background and I could just speak those wonderful words, "Come follow me, said the Lord. Be at peace within my care...."

Reading would be so much less intimidating. But when I reached for the telephone with my plan for strategic escapism, I froze.

An angel fish had landed squarely on my right shoulder and was whispering in my ear. *You can't chicken out. This is not like you.*

But then a piranha spoke up from my left shoulder. *Don't embarrass yourself or the entire choir! Let one of the others with a better voice take the part. You don't have to be a showboat. Remember the Titanic!*

They flapped their faces until I wanted to fillet them both.

Sunday morning dawned. The chances hovered somewhere around 100 percent that services would be held just as they had been for 150 years at the little white church. There was no way out, short of lying and feigning illness.

Don't you dare! Angel Fish scolded.

I was fixing my hair when she spoke up again. *It says in the Bible to make a joyful noise. If that is what it is, then just do it!*

While the anxiety did not vanish entirely, it eased. On the way to church, I prayed a simple prayer that at the very least I would not make a mistake, and at the most I might sing those few little verses well enough that someone in the congregation would be touched by the sincerity of the words. I even had a specific person in mind, Marian, who had only recently undergone a mastectomy. For her and through her, to my own sister who had also recently endured a mastectomy, I wanted there to be a blessing.

Before the choir moved to the front of the sanctuary, I remembered how all those long years ago my heart would have tried to flee by banging its way out between my ribs. I remembered clattering knees and unsteady hands. But strangely none of that was happening this time. Instead, in spite of having swallowed warm water to keep my throat clear and moist, my vocal chords were suddenly and undeniably clogged with pond sediment.

As the accompanist began the prelude, I could not so much as swallow. Her eight measures evaporated and my seventeen began.

"*'Come follow me,' said the Lord. 'Be at peace within my care,'*" the lyrics intoned. I was doing my best but I had absolutely no idea how it sounded on the other side of the microphone. Were those pained expressions on the faces of parishioners?

"Be as a child. Show me your need...." At that precise moment, a beautiful toddler let loose with a gusty squeal at the back of the sanctuary. He certainly was taking the words quite literally.

"Take my hand and I will lead." I was reaching for that hand. Was it there to latch onto?

Then just like that, my solo was over and the choir completed the song to the applause of the congregation. Patti glanced over at me and winked.

I can't ever remember a time when I have received more hugs and compliments in one morning than that Sunday in June 2002. But the very best of all was when Marian wrapped her arms around me and said, "I was just so thrilled when I saw you at the microphone. And when you sang..." She paused a moment, her eyes brimming with tears, "I just felt such a joy in my heart!"

Any of my fellow choir members could have sung those seventeen simple measures and brought joy to their fellow-churchgoers. But none perhaps, could have had them mean quite as much as they did to me that day.

I am content to be an ordinary fish in an ordinary pond. If my joyful noise makes even so much as a small splash now and then, it's good enough for me if it's good enough for Him.

He is, after all, the master fisherman.

*"Come, Follow Me," by Elly & Steve Kupferschmid, Harold Flammer, Inc.

Pennies from Heaven?

Some folks believe that when you find a penny it means your guardian angel is close by. I even read once about a guy who consistently found pennies in his shoes each morning after his wife passed away. He was convinced she had sent them to let him know she was near and was watching over him.

That seemed a bit far-fetched to me, but if he believed it and felt reassured by it, who was I to judge?

But after my father died, pennies began turning up. At first there wasn't anything as impressive as a penny in my shoe each morning, but they did manage to appear in places and in ways that could not be as easily explained as change easily dropped from a pocket at a check-out line or ticket counter.

As the years have gone by, they continue to show up repeatedly in the same places or in special new and otherwise unlikely places. A single penny appears now and then on the clothes dryer between loads of laundry, for example, when I've emptied no change from any pockets.

When I came out of a store one day in a mood so glum I thought nothing could cheer me, five new pennies gleamed against the dark pavement immediately outside the door of my car. I knew for certain they hadn't been there when I got out of the car to go into the store, because I had deliberately checked to be sure I wasn't putting my foot into a glob of gum or a splotch of motor oil when I opened my car door.

When I saw the pennies I began to laugh out loud. My angel must have known it would take more than one penny to lift me out of the doldrums that day!

On another occasion, I was walking the same route I often take from a parking lot to a camera shop in downtown Battle Creek. Curiously, I felt strangely compelled to cross the street at a point that was out of my way. As I did, I glanced down at the precise moment there was a penny in my path. It was not just lying there bright and bold as if to shout "HERE I AM!" but was wedged on its side in a crack in the pavement. What were the chances of it being spotted in such an obscure place? My angel was cleverly testing my powers of observation.

Just days later, I found a penny in my own yard nestled in the grass next to one of the tall evergreens my father had always admired.

Then, there was the morning I was feeling quite anxious about meeting an intimidating, prospective new client. His assistant escorted me to a conference room to await his arrival and motioned for me to take a specific seat at the conference table, while she went to get coffee. I reached to pull back an executive chair immediately next to where she had suggested I sit, so that I could set my briefcase on it long enough to remove some presentation materials. There, in the very center of the seat was a bright, brand new penny.

My jitters went away, the meeting went smoothly, and as it ended, I glanced at the penny beside me and whispered, "Thank you, Daddy."

Dad's angelic attention got even better the July morning in 2002 some seven years after his death, when my mother, our friend Lucille, my husband, and I set out for a week's trip to Ontario. It was barely eight a.m. when we crossed the Blue Water Bridge at Port Huron, Michigan, separating the States from Canada. Traffic had been sparse, and when we pulled in at the tidy brick building just over the border where we needed to exchange currency, there was nary another vehicle in the neat, clean parking lot. My husband parked our van nearly in the center of the lot. We were all eager to climb out and stretch after three hours on the road in the wee hours of the morning.

I slid open the side panel-door to help my mother out of the van. She held onto my arm with one hand and prepared to steady herself on her cane with the other. As she stepped from the van and leaned on the cane, her eye caught a bright gleam in the early morning sun. No more than a few inches from the tip of her cane was a brand new Canadian penny. She stooped to pick it up, holding it out to me with a smile that knew no bounds.

I had always known my dad was an above-average kind of guy. Now I know he can even be an above-average kind of angel and send his greetings in the local currency!

But one of the most special ways that pennies from heaven have made their way into my life happened on a crisp October 2002 morning when friends and family gathered for the annual Southwest Michigan Komen Race for the Cure®. Our team was raising money to honor my sister Sue as she battled breast cancer.

As I scurried around, tucking the last of our team's signage, shirts, and race forms into the car before leaving, I was stopped in my tracks by the clear and unmistakable urge to go back into the house. As surely as if the words had been spoken aloud, came the message, "*Give everyone a penny!*"

I grabbed a handful of pennies for the thirty members of our team.

"What's this for?" team members asked as I pressed a penny to their palms before the race.

"Just a little something sent by an angel!" I replied with a wink.

Dad was a part of "Team: We Love Sue" that day.

There wasn't a doubt in my mind.

Just a Little Sign

One of my mother's greatest passions is gardening. She loves to get her hands in the soil and see plants flourish, tending them with love as she has her five children, six grandchildren and five great-grandchildren.

Despite age and arthritis, Mom is always busy, always helping out, never complaining. Convincing her to put down the hoe before she is good and ready, can be a challenge even though these days she has to use the hoe as much for support as for garden work.

"I can't quit until I finish this row," she will say and minutes later, when you thought she was about to the end of the row of peas or beans and should be about finished for the day, she has completed that one, turned, and started back across the garden on another row. She does what she does out of love and says she feels close to God when she is working in the garden.

One spring day some years ago, after working practically non-stop for hours on her hands and knees in one of my flower beds, loosening the soil with a three-tined digger to get at tenacious quack grass roots, she finally took a break and came indoors for a cup of tea.

As she washed her hands, I noticed that she winced a bit when she rubbed the bar of soap between them.

"What's wrong, Mom?" I asked, knowing that if I didn't ask she wouldn't tell.

She extended her right hand for me to take a look.

There, almost in the center of her palm, was a perfectly heart-shaped blister.

True to her nature, she didn't complain, only grinned, leaned her head against my shoulder and said, "Just a little sign that I love you!"

Furious Wind

wind furious west wind
badgers branches
throws weakened limbs
mercilessly to the ground
roar like a freight train
basement is safe
lights flicker once, twice
three times
out
television black
computer blank
telephone dead
house dark
Transformation

heat glorious wood heat
embraces hearth
warms chilled limbs
mercifully to the bone
rain beats on windows
basement is snug
flames flicker once, twice
three times
glow
cat purrs
dog yawns
kettle steams
quilt comforts
Tranquility

70 mph straight line winds
Followed by loss of trees and power
October 2001

The Stone Wall

Oh the stories they could tell
these mighty stones
the hands that laid them

Oh the power that formed this land
these mighty stones
The God Who made them

wind and rain
sand and sea
eons and centuries
eternity

my life but a moment
the world merely dust
He alone knows my purpose
How can I not trust?

Oh the stories they could tell
these mighty stones
the hands that laid them

Oh the power that formed this land
these mighty stones
The God Who made them

Long Island 1998
At the *Guideposts* Writers Workshop